Testimonia for the *Bstod-pa brgyad-cu-pa*
An Early Hymn
Praising Dīpaṃkaraśrījñāna (Atiśa)

HELMUT EIMER

Testimonia for the *Bstod-pa brgyad-cu-pa*
An Early Hymn
Praising Dīpaṃkaraśrījñāna (Atiśa)

Lumbini
2003

LUMBINI INTERNATIONAL RESEARCH INSTITUTE

LUMBINI STUDIES IN BUDDHIST LITERATURE, 1

Lumbini International Research Institute
P.O.Box 39
Bhairahawa, Dist. Rupandehi
NEPAL
e-mail: liri@mos.com.np

Cover: Inscription on the Aśoka pillar in Lumbini
Photograph: LIRI

ISBN 99933-769-5-7

First published 2003
Printed in Nepal

Contents

It is a pleasure for me to express my gratitude to all who helped me in the preparation and publication of this brief work: Dr Franz-Karl Ehrhard, Research Fellow of the Lumbini International Research Institute (LIRI), Lumbini, Nepal, located the early edition of the *Bstod-pa brgyad-cu-pa* from Mang-yul Gung-thang among the treasures of Tibetan texts filmed by the Nepal-German Manuscript Preservation Project and made a copy of it accessible to me. Mrs Saralā Mānandhar, Chief, The National Archives, Kathmandu, granted permission to publish the text [NGMPP reel no. L 784/2]. Mrs. Susanne Kammüller M.A. corrected my English. Dr Christoph Cüppers, the Director of the LIRI, Lumbini, Nepal, kindly accepted this study for publication.

0. After A.D. 842, when the Tibetan kingdom had collapsed, continuing civil quarrels lead to the situation that Buddhism did not receive the necessary protection and subsidies any more; it survived, however, on a low, limited scale, especially in private houses. From the last quarter of the Xth century, the religion of the Buddha was slowly and step by step restored. This "later propagation" (*phyi-dar*) started from two sides, on the one hand from small principalities of Eastern Tibet, where Buddhism had remained the established religion, and on the other hand from the enthusiastic Buddhist kings whose realms originated in the westernmost part of Tibet after the fall of the central power.

0.1 An important impulse for religious development was given by the invitation of the Indian monk-scholar Dīpaṃkaraśrījñāna (A.D. 982-1054) to Western Tibet, where he arrived in A.D. 1042. There Atiśa —the honorific title by which he is commonly known today— met the most influential Tibetan translator Rin-chen bzang-po (A.D. 958-1055), overcame him in a debate and thereby made him his follower. When Dīpaṃkaraśrījñāna was about to return to India, the road through Nepal was blocked by a local feud. The Buddhist dignitaries of Central Tibet, who had their roots in Eastern Tibet, utilized this opportunity and commissioned 'Brom-ston Rgyal-ba'i 'byung-gnas (A.D. 1005-1064) to invite the teacher to Central Tibet, where he spent the rest of his life. Thus Atiśa became recognized by both, the western and eastern groups in the *phyi dar*, as one of the foremost spiritual leaders.

0.2 After Atiśa had passed away, his main pupil, 'Brom-ston Rgyal-ba'i 'byung-gnas, founded Rva-sgreng Monastery in A.D. 1056. It soon became the centre of the Bka'-gdams-pa ("Bound by Command"), a small order that strove to restore a more disciplined practice of religious life. The second half of the XIth century saw the emergence of two other important schools, viz. the Sa-skya-pa, and the Bka'-brgyud-pa — the Rnying-ma-pa Order, however, claimed direct descent from earlier Indian yogin-sages, especially from Padmasambhava. Later, in the beginning XVth century, when Tsong-kha-pa Blo-bzang grags-pa (A.D. 1357-1419) founded his Ribo Dga'-ldan-pa Order, he insisted on proper monastic discipline so that the Dge-lugs-pa ("the Virtuous ones") appeared as a continuation of the Bka'-gdams-pa, the Bka'-gdams-pa gsar-ma ("the New Bka'-gdams-pa").[1] Thus, Dīpaṃkaraśrījñāna became one of the Indian teachers of the most influential Dge-lugs-pa Order of Tibetan Buddhism. The brief didactic poem *Byang-chub lam-gyi sgron-ma*,[2] composed by Atiśa during his stay in Western Tibet, was one of the basic works of the Bka'-gdams-pa and the Dge-lugs-pa Orders, which was frequently referred to in early *lam-rim* treatises.[3]

1. In Buddhist literature we have many examples of eulogies on the Buddha, on eminent *guru*s, or on succession lines of teachers. On Dīpaṃkaraśrījñāna, we have a number of such hymns written already by his contemporaries. Of the eulogy written by Rin-chen bzang-po, eight lines are still preserved in quotations.[4] The most popular one today is the *Bstod-pa sum-cu-pa*, the "hymn consisting of thirty stanzas", attributed by tradition to 'Brom-ston Rgyal-ba'i 'byung-gnas; it is contained in almost all *chos-spyod*[5] collections used by Tibetan monastic communities. It refers in its main body to the founding of Rva-sgreng Monastery in the year 1056.[6]

---

[1] The two extensive histories of the Bka'-gdams-pa school utilized in this paper, viz. the *Bka'-gdams chos-'byung rnam-thar* and the *Bka'-gdams chos-'byung sgron-me* were written at a time when the Dge-lugs-pa Order already prevailed.

[2] Edited in EIMER 1978 (original Sanskrit title *Bodhipathapradīpa*).

[3] So, e.g., in the *Dam-chos yid-bzhin-gyi nor-bu thar-pa rin-po-che'i rgyan zhes-bya-ba theg-pa chen-po'i lam-rim-gyi bshad-pa* of Dvags-po Lha-rje Sgam-po-pa, cf. GUENTHER 1959: *passim*. Quotations are also found in Tsong-kha-pa's *lam-rim* compendia.

[4] Two lines in the *Bka'-gdams chos-'byung sgron-me*, fol. 56a5, and these two and six more lines in the *Bka'-gdams chos-'byung rnam-thar*, fol. 40a7-8, cf. EIMER 1977: 137-138, note 1, and EIMER 1997: 21.

[5] EIMER 1992: 183-184, knows of seven such collections containing the *Bstod-pa sum-cu-pa*.

[6] EIMER 1977: 150-152 (Quellen E 6), gives further details.

1.1 Atiśa's main Tibetan translator Nag-tsho Tshul-khrims rgyal-ba,[7] who accompanied the master for nineteen years in all from the invitation in India up to his stay in Snye-thang, wrote the *Bstod-pa brgyad-cu-pa*, the "hymn in eighty [lines / stanzas]", on the reverse of a painted scroll short time after the demise of the master, i.e. in A.D. 1054 or 1055. This is obvious from several biographies or biographical accounts on the life of Dīpaṃkaraśrījñāna;[8] the passages in question can be summed up as follows:

> About ten months before Atiśa's end, the teacher advised Nag-tsho Tshul-khrims rgyal-ba to go to meet the Pandit Jñānākara in Nepal to receive special teachings concerning Guhyasamāja (*'phags skor)*. Nag-tsho raised some objections against this, but the teacher insisted. So the Lotsāba obeyed the order of his master and went to Nepal.[9]
>
> When Nag-tsho Tshul-khrims rgyal-ba learned that Dīpaṃkaraśrījñāna had passed away, he made the artisan Kṛṣṇapa prepare a painted scroll of considerable size.[10] Above he had painted the Yi-dam gods and —in a second line— the twelve teachers of Atiśa; in the centre the master in his actual size was given and below his main Tibetan pupils. On the reverse of that scroll Nag-tsho Tshul-khrims rgyal-ba wrote the *Bstod-pa brgyad-cu-pa*. Later on, the scroll was preserved in the temple of Yang-thog.[11]

1.2 This painted scroll depicting the main events in the life of Dīpaṃkaraśrījñāna is not accessible at present. It seems, however, to have been the prototype of the thankas known today that are kept in several famous museums.[12] These scrolls differ from the one described by the biographies: they show, in the uppermost line, Ami-

---

[7] Born 1011, cf. *Bka'-gdams chos-'byung sgron-me*, fol. 67b2 (*lcags mo lug la sku 'khrungs*).

[8] EIMER 1977: 41-154, describes the 44 biographical sources on the life of Atiśa known at that time.

[9] For this passage cf. EIMER 1979: para. 393.

[10] The report speaks of *khru bcu drug*, i.e. of "sixteen cubits" size of the cotton cloth on which the thanka was painted.

[11] This passage relies on the *Bka'-gdams chos-'byung sgron-me*, fol. 67b6-68a2 (the same appears in the *Lam-rnam*, *nga* (4), fol. 181a6-b3), cf. EIMER 1979: para. 424.

[12] Cf., e.g., PAL / TSENG 1970: 46, no. 30, and plate 30.

tābha flanked by Śākyamuni (left hand side) and Avalokiteśvara (right hand side) and in the second line Tārā (left hand side) and Acala (right hand side); between this group of the Bka'-gdams lha bzhi ("the four gods of the Bka'-gdams-pa school") and Atiśa a *mchod rten* is depicted. In addition, the accessible thankas seem to contain some scenes that are not given in the early biographies going back to Nag-tsho Tshul-khrims-rgyal-ba. In any case the *Bstod-pa brgyad-cu-pa* is not preserved on the reverse side of any of the presently known scrolls. On account of the close connection of the eulogy and the painted scroll depicting the life of Atiśa, it seems probable that this hymn of praise contains some basic biographic data.

1.3 In the transmission of the life of Dīpaṃkaraśrījñāna the Lotsāba Nag-tsho Tshul-khrims rgyal-ba plays an important part: the two early detailed biographies accessible today, viz. the *Rnam-thar rgyas-pa*[13] and the *Rnam-thar yongs-grags*,[14] rely mainly on him. These two, as well as the two extensive Bka'-gdams histories, viz. the *Bka'-gdams chos-'byung rnam-thar*[15] and the *Bka'-gdams chos-'byung sgron-me*[16], comprise extensive passages that reflect the colophon of the earliest source of this biographical tradition; this can be summed up as follows:

> Some time after Dīpaṃkaraśrījñāna had passed away, Rong-pa Lag[17]-sor-pa searched for the correct teachings of the master. So he asked seven direct disciples of Atiśa and two indirect ones. While the direct pupils agreed in their explanations and accounts of the life of the teacher, the two indirect ones did not. Facing this, Rong-pa Lag-sor-pa considered that he should put his request for the teachings and the bio-

13 Full title: *Jo-bo-rje dpal-ldan mar-me-mdzad ye-shes-kyi rnam-thar rgyas-pa* (siglum **L**).

14 Full title: *Jo-bo rin-po-che dpal-ldan a-ti-sha'i rnam-thar rgyas-pa yongs-grags* (siglum **R**).

15 Full title: *Bka'-gdams rin-po-che'i chos-'byung rnam-thar nyin-mor byed-pa'i 'od-stong*, written by Bsod-nams Lha'i dbang-po in A.D. 1484 (siglum **H**).

16 Full title: *Bka'-gdams-kyi rnam-par thar-pa bka'-gdams chos-'byung gsal-ba'i sgron-me*, written by Las-chen Kun-dga' rgyal-mtshan in A.D. 1494 or 1505 (siglum **G**).

17 This syllable appears in the form *phyag* as well.

graphy before Nag-tsho Tshul-khrims rgyal-ba. This important Lotsāba did no more stay in the central area of the Dbus province but lived in Khab in the northern part of Mang-yul Gung-thang. The Lotsāba told him that he had followed Atiśa for nineteen years, that it was he who invited the master to Tibet and that so far no one had come to ask questions concerning Dīpaṃkaraśrījñāna. Later on —in this connection the span of 21 years is mentioned— four monks, viz. Dge-bshes Zul-phu-ba Bya 'Dul-ba 'dzin-pa,[18] Rog Mching-phu-ba, Gnam-par-ba[19] and Dge-bshes Zhu-len-pa, and a novice became pupils of Rong-pa Lag-sor-pa with the aim of obtaining instructions as for the teachings[20] and the life of Atiśa. The written notes of his co-pupils eventually came into the hands of Zul-phu-ba 'Dul-ba 'dzin-pa, who composed from them the extensive account[21] of Atiśa's life.[22]

1.4 The original version of this first extensive biography apparently did not survive. The *Rnam-thar rgyas-pa*, accessible only in an 18th century block print edition prepared in Dga'-ldan phun-tshogs gling, seems to follow it very closely, as we deduce from a remarkable number of archaic syntactical structures used. On account of many similar and even corresponding passages, the *Rnam-thar yongs-grags* written by Mchims Nam-mkha'-grags (1210-1285)[23] can be regarded as a modernized version of the "extensive account of Atiśa's life" (*lo-rgyus chen-mo*).[24] Hence follows that the *Rnam-*

---

18 A.D. 1100-1174 or 1091-1166; the former date is given by Las-chen Kun-dga' rgyal-mtshan in his *Bka'-gdams chos-'byung sgron-me*, fol. 337b5 and 338a5, the latter by 'Gos Lo-tsā-ba Gzhon-nu-dpal in his *Deb-ther sngon-po*, cf. ROERICH 1949-53: I, 80.

19 According to 'Gos Lo-tsā-ba Gzhon-nu-dpal, *Deb-ther sngon-po* (cf. ROERICH 1949-53: I, 328f.), Abbot of Gsang-phu Monastery 1143-1151.

20 Each of the four pupils of Rong-pa Lag-sor-pa wrote his own *Bstan-rim* as pointed out in the *Deb-ther dmar-po*, cf. JACKSON 1996: 239-240.

21 The biographies speak of *lo-rgyus*, *jo-bo'i lo-rgyus*, (*jo-bo'i*) *lo-rgyus chen-mo*, or *jo-bo'i lam-yig* side by side.

22 This summary relies mainly on the *Bka'-gdams chos-'byung sgron-me*, fol. 336a5-337b5. A German version of the passage in question with the main parallels is given in EIMER 1977: 279-291 (paras 7.2.-7.2.9.), cf. EIMER 1979: paras 438-443.

23 Cf. VAN DER KUIJP 1996: 46.

24 EIMER 1977: 234-236, paras 5.3.1.1.-5.3.2., comes to the end that the

thar rgyas-pa —maybe in a slightly different form— and the *Rnam-thar yongs-grags*[25] reflect the biography as it existed at the middle or the end of the 13th century, even if each text contains textual material of its own.

1.5 Thus, the origin of the prose biographies and that of the *Bstod-pa brgyad-cu-pa* are closely connected with the Lotsāba Nag-tsho Tshul-khrims rgyal-ba. This is corroborated by the fact that both the *Rnam-thar rgyas-pa* and the *Rnam-thar yongs-grags* several times quote eulogistic verses by titles like *Lo-tsā-ba'i Bstod-pa brgyad-cu-pa* or *Lo-tsā-ba'i Bstod-pa* for confirming accounts of Dīpaṃkaraśrījñāna's life. The *Bka'-gdams chos-'byung sgron-me* contains many verses from the *Bstod-pa brgyad-cu-pa* which are not recorded elsewhere in the prose transmission of Atiśa's life;[26] it seems to rely on a comprehensive version of the eulogy. In addition, the *Bka'-gdams chos-'byung sgron-me* comprises further quotations from different sources. Some verses of the *Bstod-pa brgyad-cu-pa* appear in manuals of the "graded path" (*lam rim*) as well, starting with Tsong-kha-pa's famous *Lam-rim chen-mo*. But we also find them in commentaries on Atiśa's *Bodhipathapradīpa*, e.g., in the *Lam-sgron rnam-bshad*[27] of Blo-bzang Chos-kyi rgyal-mtshan, the Paṇ-chen Lama I (1567-1662).

---

colophon at the end of the *Rnam-thar yongs-grags* merely adopted the name Mchims Thams-cad mkhyen-pa, i.e. Mchims Nam-mkha'-grags; this cannot regarded as being correct any more. The *Bka'-gdams glegs-bam* which comprises the *Rnam-thar yongs-grags* was after a span of time of oral transmission finally redacted in A.D. 1302 by 'Brom-ston Kumāramati (Tibetan: Gzhon-nu blo-gros), cf. EHRHARD 2002: 44.

25 At present five editions of the *Bka'-gdams glegs-bam* are known, four of them have been used for the analysis of the biographical sources on Atiśa, cf. EIMER 1977: 71-80, and EIMER 1979: part 1, 37-42. The earliest block print edition was prepared in A.D. 1538, cf. EHRHARD 2000: 42-45 (paras 9. to 9.2).

26 Lines 54-57, 71-86, 91-106, 121-124, 137-142, 149-152, 175-176, 189-245, 252-255, 264-267, 272-275, 295-302, 309-310, 315-318, 323-324, 326-332, 337-352, and 361-363.

27 Full title: *Byang-chub lam-gyi sgron-ma'i rnam-bshad phul-byung bzhad-pa'i dga'-ston* (siglum **P**).

2. Apparently only very few manuscripts or blockprint editions, be it in collections, be it in the form of separate books, existed of the *Bstod-pa brgyad-cu-pa*. It has not been described so far in any catalogues or lists of collections of Tibetan books. There is only one reference to it in a *dkar chag* of a printing house, viz. in that of the A-mchog Dga'-ldan chos-'khor-gling, which has been edited by R. O. MEISEZAHL.[28] But, a copy of the seven folio edition of our hymn of praise has not yet become accessible.

2.1 One edition of the *Bstod-pa brgyad-cu-pa*, comprising 363 lines of verse, is contained in a collection of Bka'-gdams-pa texts entitled *Bang-mdzod*.[29] According to a note in the general colophon of that book, the editors relied on textual sources belonging to the famous Tibetan polymath of the 19th century, 'Jam- dbyangs Mkhyen-brtse dbang-po (1820-1892).[30] Therefore it cannot have been prepared before the second half of the 19th century. A diplomatic transliteration of the eulogy on Atiśa contained in the *Bang-mdzod* was published under the title: “Nag tsho Tshul khrims rgyal ba's Bstod pa brgyad cu pa in Its Extant Version” by the present writer in 1989.

2.2 Recently Dr Franz-Karl Ehrhard located a six folio block print with the title *Jo-bo-rje'i bstod-pa brgyad-cu-pa nag-tsho lo-tstshā-ba tshul-khrims rgyal-bas mdzad pa* among the Tibetan literary treasures microfilmed by the Nepal-German Manuscript Preservation Project. It was prepared in Mang-yul Gung-thang[31] in the year A.D. 1541,[32] as Dr Ehrhard interprets its —incomplete— final printers' colophon. Therefore, it is much older than the edition of the *Bstod-pa brgyad-cu-pa* in the *Bang-mdzod*.

---

[28] MEISEZAHL 1986: 322, Nr. 55.

[29] Full title: *Legs-par bshad-pa bka'-gdams rin-po-che'i gsung-gi gces-btus nor-bu'i bang-mdzod*, our eulogy is found on fol. 15b1-20a5.

[30] This name is given in the colophon on fol. 295b6.

[31] A first comprehensive study of these early block prints gives EHRHARD 2000.

[32] This means that it was printed shortly after the *Bka'-gdams glegs-bam*, cf. above note 25.

2.3 In the colophon to the edition of the *Bstod-pa brgyad-cu-pa*, which appears fol. 5a2 of the Mang-yul Gung-thang xylograph, we read the following:

> *ces khams gsum chos kyi rgyal po | dpal ldan mar me mdzad ye shes la bstod pa'i rab tu byed pa |* ***tshig rkang*** *brgyad cu pa zhes bya ba | nag tsho lo tstsha ba tshul rgyal bas sbyar ba rdzogs sho | |*
> "The presentation of the praise of Dpal-ldan Mar-me-mdzad (Śrīmad Dīpaṃkara), the *Dharmarāja* of the three spheres, with the title 'That one Consisting of Eighty Lines of Verse', which was composed by Nag-tsho Lotsāba Tshul[-khrims] rgyal-ba, is finished."

2.4 The version of the corresponding colophon given at the end of the *Bstod-pa brgyad-cu-pa* as contained in the *Bang-mdzod*, however, differs in one major point, namely, that it reads *tshigs-bcad* "stanza" instead of *tshig-rkang* "line of verse".[33] Thus, the title of the eulogy is to be translated "That one Consisting of Eighty Stanzas". The difference between the colophons leads to the question whether the old *Bstod-pa brgyad-cu-pa* comprised 80 stanzas or only 80 lines of verse. The two available editions of the eulogy, however, cover more than 360 lines of verse in all. The standard stanza in general consists of four lines of verse, that would mean that the full number should reach 320 lines if we disregard that in some cases six or even eight lines are taken together to form a stanza. Considering the number of 363 lines in the text as we know it now, the title "That one Consisting of Eighty Stanzas" could therefore be correct. But, as a matter of fact, the *Bang-mdzod* edition of the *Bstod-pa brgyad-cu-pa* contains, after line 25, a gloss saying that the lines preceding are regarded by the authors of the *Bka'-gdams chos-'byung rnam-thar* and the *Bka'-gdams chos-'byung sgron-me* as composed by Paṇḍita Sa'i snying-po. This is corroborated by the introductions to the quotations of the verses in question in other sources as well.[34]

---

33 LOKESH CHANDRA 1992-94: 6, 1519a, s.v. *tshig-rkang* gives as Sanskrit equivalent *pada*.

34 Cf. below para. 4.1.

2.5 In face of the unsolved question concerning the authorship of the individual stanzas, this paper presents the text of the *Bstod-pa brgyad-cu-pa* relying on the Gung-thang xylograph in a diplomatic edition without any emendation.[35] The apparatus records the readings[36] occurring in the text as extant in the *Bang-mdzod* and in the quotations given by the known major prose sources for the life of Dīpaṃkaraśrījñāna. In addition to the locations of individual quotations, their introductions are noted as well in order to give the reader all necessary information as to the specific lines referred to by the biographical sources. The translation of some stanzas in this paper relies on those readings that best suit the contents; these are given without any further notice.

2.6 In spite of its age, the Mang-yul Gung-thang xylograph is not superior in its readings to the *Bang-mdzod* edition. This is obvious from the fact, e.g., that lines 94 and 331 of the 363 lines in that early xylograph are missing; in preparing the blocks for printing the omission of a further line was noticed and an appropriate correction was made.[37] On the other hand, there is a reading in the Gung-thang xylograph that points to Old Tibetan orthography, viz., *brtul-shugs* instead of standard Tibetan *brtul-zhugs* in line 49. Thus, we have at hand two textual witnesses for the *Bstod-pa brgyad-cu-pa* besides the testimonia for individual stanzas in the form of quotations.[38]

---

[35] The texts which follow the *Bstod-pa brgyad-cu-pa* in the Mang-yul Gung-thang block print are simply transliterated without any comment. They contain fol. 5a3-5 a brief prayer, fol. 5a5-5b3 the eulogy on "The Reverend Teacher from Bengal", i.e. on Atiśa, by Lha bla-ma Byang-chub-'od, fol. 5b3-7 the *Sangs-rgyas-kyi mdzad-pa bcu-gnyis-kyi bstod-pa* by Slob-dpon Dpa'-bo, and fol. 6a1-7 a eulogy on a line of eminent Buddhist teachers.

[36] Reference to the critical notes is made by exponent numbers referring to the preceding syllable or syllables as far as it / they are given in italics in the text.

[37] Starting from the third syllable of line 119 to the end of line 121 the letters appear squeezed, this indicates that in the master copy for cutting the block or in the original version of the block something was missing.

[38] Unattested by the biographical sources utilized here are two single lines, viz. 9 and 325, and eight groups of lines, viz. 26-33, 107-110, 125-126, 256-

2.7 A relatively close connection between the quotations in the *Bka'-gdams chos-'byung sgron-me* and the text of our eulogy in the *Bang-mdzod* edition can be established: the intermediate gloss after line 25 says that Bsod-nams lha'i dbang-po and Las-chen Kun-dga' rgyal-mtshan refer to Sa'i snying-po as the author of the preceding lines. Thus, it is obvious that their historical works were consulted for preparing the edition of our hymn in the *Bang-mdzod*. There is a remarkable number of identical readings in the quotations given by the *Bka'-gdams chos-'byung sgron-me* and the *Bstod-pa brgyad-cu-pa* in the *Bang-mdzod*.[39] The fact that we do not have as many identical variants between the *Bka'-gdams chos-'byung rnam-thar* and the *Bang-mdzod* is very easily explained: Bsod-nams lha'i dbang-po quotes only a limited number of lines from the eulogy — besides, his book exists only in a *dbu-med* manuscript. In an additional line after line 360, the *Bka'-gdams chos-'byung sgron-me* refers to the "picture of the *guru*" because its author was aware of the origin of the *Bstod-pa brgyad-cu-pa*, which was written first on the reverse of a painted scroll showing Dīpaṃkaraśrījñāna.

2.8 At two points, the *Rnam-thar rgyas-pa* reads a Sanskrit term instead of its Tibetan equivalent against all other textual witnesses, viz. in line 161 *lo-ka* instead of *'jig-rten* ("world") and in line 268 *duḥ-kha* instead of *sdug-bsngal* ("suffering"). In one case this archaic biography interprets the word *rab-byung*[40] by adding two syllables: *rab-tu byung-ba* "monk" expresses the intended meaning of that line, but it does not suit the seven-syllable metre. The *Rnam-thar rgyas-pa*, against the other textual evidence, comprises seven syllables after the quotation of lines 24-25 saying "I pay [my] rever-

---

259, 293-294, 303-308, 311-314, and 353-360. Thus, as long as the comprehensive versions of the *Bstod-pa brgyad-cu-pa* were not accessible, it was not possible to reconstruct the complete text.

39 It has to be noted here that the *Bka'-gdams chos-'byung sgron-me* quotes more than 85 percent of the whole *Bstod-pa brgyad-cu-pa*.

40 This word has two meanings, viz., (1.) "the 60 year cycle of the calendar" or "its first year" and (2.) "one who has left the house to become a monk".

ence to Atiśa"; this line could originally have been the final clause of the Sa'i sning-po hymn. Two further additions are found after line ten and as a substitute for lines 88 and 89.[41]

2.9 The readings culled from the accessible text witnesses for the *Bstod-pa brgyad-cu-pa* do not permit to draw a picture of the transmission of that hymn.[42] It is not possible to establish a connection between the Mang-yul Gung-thang and the *Bang-mdzod* edition. We have to assume that the quotations as given in the *Lam-rim chen-mo*, in the *Bka'-gdams chos-'byung rnam-thar*, in the *Bka'-gdams chos-'byung sgron-me*, etc. derive from sources which were among the forerunners of the extensive biographical reports on Dīpaṃkaraśrījñāna presently accessible. Besides, we do not know whether or not the *Bstod-pa brgyad-cu-pa* was used in the rituals of the early times.[43]

3. A preliminary investigation into the individual stanzas contained in the transmitted text of the *Bstod-pa brgyad-cu-pa* must search for possible breaks in the structure of the poem. We can, e.g., rely on a change of metre or on differences between the contents and the character of individual stanzas or groups of stanzas. As for variations in metre, we find that the majority of lines count seven syllables, only eight four-line stanzas are in the nine-syllable metre, viz. lines 26-49, 333-336 and 353-356.

3.1 The first block of six stanzas (viz. lines 26-49) starts with a typical introduction to a poem or hymn. The first two of them, in translation, run as follows:

---

[41] After line 10 is added: "His son was Dga'-ba'i dpal"; this separates the lines 10 and 11 which name Atiśa's father and mother. Then, after the quotation of lines 87 and 90, two lines are inserted —substituting lines 88 and 89— to form a four-lined stanza which refers to the beauty of the teacher.

[42] It is settled that the edition in the *Bang-mdzod* —as already said above— relies to some extent on the two histories of the Bka'-gdams-pa school by Bsod-nams lha'i dbang-po and Las-chen Kun-dga' rgyal-mtshan.

[43] This would mean that an oral transmission existed.

Lines 26-29

You are the source of all good qualities;[44]
as a great scholar—whose mercy is deep as the ocean
of good qualities—on account of your good qualities
I will praise you in a meaningful way.

Lines 30-33

To [you,] the father who has a wide learning
of the five fields of study,[45]
who cares for himself and for others alike,
who regards himself and others as exchangeable,
to Śrīmad Dīpaṃkara I bow in reverence.[46]

3.2 In the same manner as lines 30-33, the following four stanzas, i.e. lines 34-49, end in the refrain: ... *la phyag-'tshal-lo*, "I bow in reverence to...":

Lines 34-37

[You] neglect your own goal[47] [, but] take pain in
[caring for] the goal of others, [you] are my teacher;
to [you,] who always acts in person
or indirectly for the goal of others,
to the merciful teacher, I bow in reverence.

The three ensuing stanzas (i.e. lines 38-49) do not only end in ... *la phyag-'tshal-lo* like the preceding ones, but also share the common feature of an almost formular first line *khyod-ni* [...] *sgor zhugs-nas*, "You, after [you] had entered the door [...]"; the only variation

[44] This translates *yon-tan*, i.e. the equivalent of Sanskrit *guṇa*.

[45] The five fields of study are listed in the *Rnam-thar yongs-grags* (fol. 8a5-6) as follows (1.) *sgra* i.e. *sgra'i rig-pa / śabdavidyā*, "Grammar", (2.) *gtan-tshigs* i.e. *gtan-tshigs-kyi rig-pa / hetuvidyā*, "Logic", (3.) *bzo* i.e. *bzo'i gnas-kyi rig-pa / śilpakarmasthānavidyā*, "Art / Handicraft", (4.) *gso-ba* i.e. *gso-ba'i rig-pa / cikitsāvidyā*, "Medicine", and (5.) *nang rig-pa* i.e. *nang-gi rig-pa / adhyātmavidyā* "Buddhist Religion"; cf. EIMER 1977: 161-162 (para. 2.1.1.2.), and *Mahāvyutpatti* 1989: paras 1558-1562.

[46] No quotations of the lines 26-33 have been located anywhere.

[47] This translates *don* (Sanskrit *artha*).

being two syllables in between that give —in upward gradation— the Tibetan terms for Śrāvakayāna, Pāramitāyāna, and Mantrayāna, respectively. Together with the refrain at the end, these introductory lines constitute a conspicuous frame structure for the three stanzas; they run as follows:

Lines 38-41

After you had entered the door of the Śrāvakayāna,
you kept [to the rules of] morality
like a Yak [trying to save] his tail;
to you, the most excellent monk with perfect morality,
to the Sthavira, the Vinayadhara, I bow in reverence.

Lines 42-45

After you had entered the door of the Pāramitā[yāna],
you did not forsake the living beings due to your *bodhicitta*,
which consists of perfectly pure good intentions;
to you, the wise and merciful one, I bow in reverence.

Lines 46-49

After you had entered the door of the Mantrayāna,[48]
you possessed the *vajra* mind, regarding yourself as a god;
to you, the master of *yoga*, the Avadhūtipa,
who has taken a secret vow, I bow in reverence.

Thus, lines 26-49 contain an uninterrupted sequence of stanzas that form a coherent eulogy, with only a colophon missing. These six stanzas are obviously an insertion into the present *Bstod-pa brgyad-cu-pa*, because they differ in metre, contents, and style from the surrounding text. The preceding seven-syllable lines (i.e. 24-25) say: "Such a kingdom of Bengal, he left and went towards salvation," and lines 50-51 resume the topic of lines 1-23: "You were born in the best of families, in the family of the kings." The ensuing stanza reads in lines 55-57: "... you gave up this kingdom of Bengal like a clot of spittle and you propagated the teaching of the Buddha".

[48] The passage quoted in the *Lam-rim chen-mo* gives Vajrayāna instead.

3.3 There are —as said above— still two other stanzas in the present *Bstod-pa brgyad-cu-pa* that consist of nine-syllable lines. The first of them expressly refers to the nineteen years Nag-tsho Tshul-khrims rgyal-ba followed Atiśa in the following words:

Lines 333-336

In spite of having been for nineteen years [closely]
together with you, the teacher, the holy *(kalyāṇa)mitra*,
I never noticed a sinful defilement [arising]
which affected [your] body, speech or mind.[49]

The second of the two stanzas in question gives the name of that Lotsāba, it reads as follows:

Lines 353-356

Owing to his reverend teacher being praised
by the monk [from] Nag-tsho
[named] Tshul-khrims-rgyal-ba,
all the five [forms of] living beings
whom he loved as his own sons
shall meet [him] in the sphere of Tuṣita.[50]

It is possible that the final clause in the preceding seven-syllable stanza 349-352,[51] the wish *dga' ldan gnas su 'grogs par shog*, "... shall meet ... in the sphere of Tuṣita", attracted the lines 353-356

---

[49] This stanza appears in the *Rnam-thar yongs-grags*, fol. 84a3-4, in a shortened —seven-syllable— version, the missing syllables (two per line) are set in brackets here:

| *bla ma [dge ba'i] bshes gnyen dam pa khyed* |
| *lo ni bcu dgu bsten [cing 'grogs] na yang* |
| *[khyod kyi] sku gsung thugs kyi 'khrul pa yi* |
| *nyes pa'i dri ma [byung ba] mthong re skan* | .

[50] The final portion of the *Bstod-pa brgyad-cu-pa* starts after line 356, it contains a wishing prayer spoken by Tshul-khrims rgyal-ba, i.e. Nag-tsho Lotsāba, see below para. 7.1.

[51] Lines 349-352: "When I remember your good qualities, I shed tears and the hair on [my] body bristles. I shall meet you, reverend teacher, in the sphere of Tuṣita."

which end in the same words. The two stanzas constituted by lines 333-336[52] and 353-356[53] appear to have formed a sort of summary and colophon to the six coherent stanzas in the nine-syllable metre. So we come to the conclusion that the 32 nine-syllable lines appearing at three places in the *Bstod-pa brgyad-cu-pa* can be regarded as a eulogy of its own, which originally consisted of eight (*brgyad*) stanzas in all.

4. When we consider the character of the 25 initial lines of the poem, we find no formal introduction to the hymn, instead the text starts with a coherent narrative account describing, in plain words, the country, the home town, and the family of Dīpaṃkaraśrījñāna. The structure of this passage differs from the remainder of the poem, where sentences generally cover two or four lines and are combined to regular stanzas of four lines.[54] The following translated passage contains stanzas consisting of three or even five lines:

Lines 1-25

In the East, in the excellent country Za-hor
there is a great city.
[It] is Vikramapura.
In its centre the royal residence
is a very large palace
It is called 'that [one] with the golden banners'.
In revenue, power [and] wealth
it is equal to [that of] the king of China-Tonking;[55]

---

[52] In the *Rnam-thar rgyas-pa* (fol. 42a4-5) the quotation of lines 334 and 336 appears, only separated by a short introductory sentence, after that of lines 46-49. Thus, it seems probable that the two quotations are taken from the same source.

[53] At this instance, we should indicate that the lines 353-356 do not appear as quoted in any of the biographical sources utilized for this paper.

[54] We also find six-line stanzas covering three sentences of two lines or a sentence of four lines combined with one consisting of two lines (cf. lines 143-148, 293-298, 299-304, and 305-310).

[55] The gloss added to this line in the *Bang-mdzod* edition says: "The words *stong khun* mean 'Eastern King' in Chinese". The two syllables can be understood as meaning Tongking, a name that was in use for the main part of the

[It numbers] 27 times 100,000 houses.
The king of this country Dge-ba'i dpal [and
his] wife Dpal-mo'i 'od-zer-can,
both [as] parents had three sons:
Pa-dma'i snying[-po], Zla-ba'i snying[-po,
and] Dpal-gyi-snying-po [they were] named.
The prince Pa-dma'i snying-po had
five wives [and] nine sons,
[his] eldest son, Bsod-nams-dpal,
[is] at the present time a great scholar,
[he] is known under the name Dha-na-shri.
The middle [prince], Zla-ba'i snying-po,
is at present the venerable teacher (i.e. Atiśa).
The youngest [prince], Dpal-gyi snying-po,
is the monk Vīryacandra.
Such a kingdom of Bengal
he left and went towards salvation.

4.1 The majority of the biographies quote the lines 1-8,[56] 10-19, 22-23, 20-21, and 24-25[57] in connection with the name of the Indian scholar Sa'i snying-po, who met Dīpaṃkaraśrījñāna even some time earlier than Nag-tsho Tshul-khrims rgyal-ba. The *Bka'-gdams chos-'byung sgron-me* reports that Sa'i snying-po initially was Atiśa's companion and became his pupil after he had received some tantric instructions from him.[58] This could have happened even earlier than

---

present day Northern Vietnam; according to STEIN 1961: 29, note 70, they stand for "T'ang-kiun" which means "sovereign of T'ang".

[56] Line 9 (*khyim ni 'bum phrag nyi shu bdun*) does not appear in the quoted material, but its contents seem to belong to the early tradition, because the prose of the *Rnam-thar rgyas-pa* (fol. 22a1-2), the *Rnam-thar yongs-grags* (fol. 2b1), and the *Bka'-gdams chos-'byung rnam-thar* (fol. 21b7-8) refer to "27 times 100.000 houses" as well, cf. EIMER 1979: para. 099.

[57] Lines 24-25 are quoted only by the *Rnam-thar rgyas-pa* and the *Bka'-gdams chos-'byung sgron-me*, they are not found in the *Lam-rim chen-mo* and in the *Lam-rnam*.

[58] Fol. 64b1-2: *sngar jo bo'i grogs po yin | gsang sngags la phyi nang gi khyad par dbye dka' bar byung ba jo bos legs pas phye ste gsungs pas dad de*

A.D. 1010, at a time when the master observed only tantric practices.[59] Later on, Paṇḍita Sa'i snying-po accompanied him on his way to Tibet.[60] Of the early testimonia, only Tsong-kha-pa Blo-bzang grags-pa —and most probably depending on him Ye-shes rgyal-mtshan— attributes the lines 1-8, 10-19, 22-23, and 20-21 to Nag-tsho Lo-tsā-ba Tshul-khrims rgyal-ba's *Bstod-pa brgyad-cu-pa*.[61]

5. The extant version of the *Bstod-pa brgyad-cu-pa* comprises some further coherent narrative passages set in seven-syllable lines which in style and structure are comparable to lines 1-25. The verses in question run as follows:

Lines 58-70

At Otantapuri
[there] were 53 monks.
At Vikramaśilā
[there] were about 100 monks.
[You] have entered the four main schools completely.
[You] did not take pride in [one] school.
[You have] become in the Magadha country
in all the monasteries
for the four congregations of
the Teacher [i.e. the Buddha]
for all [of them] the crown jewel.
When [you] were residing at the head
of all the eighteen schools,
all accepted [your] instructions.

| *phyis slob mar gyur pa yin gsung*. The name Sa'i snying-po appears only once in the Bstan 'gyur, viz. as name of the man who translated the *Vajragaruḍasādhana* (Tibetan *Rdo-rje khyung-gi sgrub-thabs*) of Vajrapadma together with Rma ban, cf. *Tibetan Tripitaka* 1955-61: text no. 3042.

59 Atiśa was ordained a *bhikṣu* at the age of 29 years.

60 This is attested at several places in the biographical sources.

61 The quotation in question is introduced by: *lo tstsha ba chen pos nag tshos mdzad pa'i bstod pa brgyad cu pa* (resp. in the *Lam-rnam* by: *jo bo'i bstod pa brgyad cu pa*).

Lines 111-118

In [your] twenty-first year [of life][62]
you were learned in the sixty-four arts,
in all species of handicraft,
in the well-set language,
in all the books on phonetics
and in all [sorts of] logic.
Since you followed many a good teacher,
you were decorated with the ornament of learning.

Lines 177-193

Previously at Somapuri,
when you were teaching the Tarkajvālā,[63]
you said that in twenty years [counted from]
today you would give up the *saṃskāra*s of life.
After two years from that [time] had elapsed,
at the time of [your] departure for Tibet,
you said in Vikramaśilā:
"In eighteen years [counted from] today,[64]
after [I] have given up the *saṃskāra*s of life,
I leave this body [of mine] in Tibet".
That this happened according
to the words uttered
without an error is a great miracle.
After you had left in the country of Tibet
this body of yours [the time] of which
had ripened in Tibet,

---

62 This corresponds to A.D. 1002, when we consider the year of Dīpaṃkaraśrījñāna's birth to be A.D. 982.

63 The Tibetan translation of the *Madhyamakahṛdayavṛtti-Tarkajvālā* of Bhavya, viz. the *Dbu-ma'i snying-po'i 'grel-pa rtog-ge 'bar-ba*, was done by Dīpaṃkaraśrījñāna and (Nag-tsho) Tshul-khrims rgyal-ba, cf. *Tibetan Tripitaka* 1955-1961: text no. 5256.

64 Commonly the date of the travel to Tibet is given as A.D. 1040, but Atiśa died already in A.D. 1054. Therefore, we have to accept A.D. 1037 as the date meant here. Most probably Nag-tsho Tshul-khrims rgyal-ba was already in India at this time, cf. note 68 below.

by means of the wishing prayer this body
will be born before Maitreya in the Tuṣita heaven,
[this is] foretold by Tārā, [so it is] said.[65]

Lines 246-251
When all came together and assembled
in the Palace of Mahābodhi,[66]
[you] completely overthrew by argument,
with words [sounding like] a lion's roar,
all vain disputes on philosophical issues,
[those] of [your] own and the other schools.

Lines 276-292
When [between] the two, the king Neyapāla[67]
and the Karna king [from] the West,
a great dispute had arisen,
the Karṇa king [from] the West
led [his] army into Magadha;
without taking the city he led [it] into the monasteries,
and five persons, monks [or] novices, were killed.
Many things [he] carried off as booty.
Since you felt no anger,
you were not displeased, mercy arose [in your heart].
When the battle turned back,
[you were] a shelter for the soldiers.
Later on [you,] the teacher, prepared peace:
Except for the things [necessary] for a living
the things [taken as booty]
were entirely left behind.
Disregarding [your] body and life

---

65 To this passage the following four-line stanza (lines 194-197) appears to be attached: "[You] will be born as a son of the gods (line 195) named Nam-mkha dri[-ma] med[-pa]. [You] hear the deep and ample teaching from Maitreyanātha."

66 I.e. the present Bodh Gayā.

67 Lines 337-340 refer to the king Neyapāla as well: "The ruler of Magadha is the king Neyapāla. It is difficult to say that such [and such] are [his] wealth, retinue, power etc."

[you] crossed the great river again [and] again.
Having prepared peace [between] these two
[you] made them friends.

5.1 These narrative verses outline events of the time when Atiśa lived in India. They apply a plain language and, in addition, do not generally structure the stanzas in four lines. In this, they resemble the lines 1-25, which tradition attributes to the Paṇḍita Sa'i snying-po. But, as a matter of fact, it is possible that the lines 58-70, 111-118, 177-193, 246-251, and 276-292 were written by Nag-tsho Tshul-khrims rgyal-ba who for several years lived together with Dīpamkaraśrījñāna in India already.[68]

6. Some other passages of our eulogy that do not apply the rule that a stanza has to consist of four lines do not expressly refer to Dīpaṃkaraśrījñāna's life in India, they tell instead of the master's spiritual abilities. Here follow examples of such stanzas:

Lines 129-136
The teachers [you] always followed
[were] Śāntipa and Gser-gling-pa,
Bhadrabodhi [and] Jñānaśrī.
Out of traditions handed down in lines from one to one,
[stemming] from many who have reached *siddhi*
and especially from Nāgārjuna,
you were provided with deep and ample
religious instruction.

---

[68] The nineteen years of Nag-tsho Tshul-khrims rgyal-ba accompanying Dīpaṃkaraśrījñāna (cf. line 333) ended when the former was sent to study under Jñānākara in A.D. 1053. In calculating back we have to take into account that Tshul-khrims rgyal-ba met Atiśa already on his first journey to India; then he returned to Tibet, from where he was sent out again by the Western Tibetan king Byang-chub-'od with the request to invite the master again. This travelling to and fro should have lasted at least one full year. Therefore the first meeting with Dīpamkaraśrījñāna can date back as far as A.D. 1032.

Lines 161-168

[You] obtained the favour (or: privilege)
to see the faces of Śrīmad Hevajra and
Trisamayarāja and
the hero Lokeśvara and
the reverend Lady Tārā and others,
and [you] heard in dreams or personally
the deep and ample
holy teaching every time.

7. The majority of lines contained in the presently extant *Bstod-pa brgyad-cu-pa*, i. e. more than 200, form regular stanzas of four —or six[69]— lines. In this respect they differ from the verse passages quoted above.[70] As for their contents, they do not refer to events in the life of Atiśa, but praise the master in terms of his religious achievements, which the following examples demonstrate:[71]

Lines 198-201

Therefore you are a great [man who]
has become an ornament for Jambudvīpa.
[Your] reputation sounds well, [you] are matchless,
[you] are worthy as a teacher of scholars.

Lines 319-322

If [you], the teacher (i.e. Atiśa) had not come to Tibet,
all [people there] would have become almost blind.
Since you, [a man] of wide knowledge, came,
the sun of wisdom has risen in Tibet.

7.1. The concluding verse passage of the *Bstod-pa brgyad-cu-pa*, so to speak the final wishing prayer of the eulogy in its present form, appears —if the line only preserved in the quotation in the *Bka'-gdams chos-'byung sgron-me* is taken into the text— as a regular

---

69 Cf. note 54 above.

70 Cf. paras 4., 5., and 6. above.

71 Two examples for this are already given above para. 3., note 51 (lines 349-352), and para. 5., note 65 (lines 194-197).

eight-line stanza consisting of one coherent sentence. But it is obvious that it can also be regarded as a regular stanza consisting of two four-line sentences the first of which ends in a participle instead of a finite verb. The lines run:

Lines 357-363

With all the Eighty Stanzas,
[this] eulogy on the reverend teacher,
two pupils, three pupils[72] [and]
the other pupils shall gather in faith to you and,
[facing the picture[73] of the teacher][74]
with very faithful hearts,
shall praise you all the time
— thus prays Tshul-khrims rgyal-ba.

8. It is obvious that the *Bstod-pa brgyad-cu-pa* as we have it today comprises passages of quite differing characters which most probably originate from divergent sources.[75] We cannot detect the time at which the individual stanzas or groups of stanzas were put together into a comprehensive hymn of praise. It is quite possible that this was already done by Nag-tsho Tshul-khrims rgyal-ba in A.D. 1054 or shortly afterwards when he wrote the eulogy on the reverse of the painted scroll depicting the life of Dīpaṃkaraśrījñāna — the thanka in its remarkable size[76] offered space enough for doing so. So it is possible that the 25 initial lines were regarded at that time as part of the *Bstod-pa brgyad-cu-pa* — and this in spite of the fact that the earlier accounts of Atiśa's life have preserved Sa'i

---

[72] *Slob gsum*: most probably Khu-ston Brtson-'grus g.yung-drung, Rngog Legs-pa'i shes-rab, and 'Brom-ston Rgyal-ba'i 'byung-gnas are meant here.

[73] This refers to the painted scroll depicting Atiśa's life.

[74] This line has been taken from the only testimony, viz., the quotation given in the *Bka'-gdams chos-'byung sgron-me*.

[75] A close parallel to lines 149-156 of the *Bstod-pa brgyad-cu-pa* appears in the hymn on Atiśa by Lha bla-ma Byang-chub-'od given fol. 5a5-b3 of the Gung-thang Mang-yul xylograph (cf. above note 35). It cannot be found out at present from where these lines originate.

[76] Cf. above note 10.

snying-po as the name of the original author. In any case, these stanzas were known in A.D. 1402 as belonging to Nag-tsho Tshul-khrims rgyal-ba's hymn on Atiśa, as the introduction to the quotation in Tsong-kha-pa's *Lam-rim chen-mo* attests.[77]

8.1 The name Nag-tsho Tshul-khrims rgyal-ba appears not only in the title and the colophon of the *Bstod-pa brgyad-cu-pa*, but the final wishing prayers at the end of the hymn (viz. lines 353 and 363) give his name, too. The introductions to the other verses quoted are of no help in identifying the original authors: in several instances we find the author mentioned simply by the title Lotsāba instead of the name Nag-tsho Tshul-khrims rgyal-ba, in the majority of cases the source for the stanzas of our hymn is labelled "[*Bstod pa*] *Brgyad-cu-pa*", "(*Dge-bshes*) *Lo-tsā[tstshā]-ba'i bstod-pa*",[78] or simply "*Bstod-pa*". Therefore we need to come to the conclusion that it is impossible to identify with any certainty the specific authors of the individual stanzas of the *Bstod-pa brgyad-cu-pa* — as long as no sources going back to earliest times become accessible.

---

[77] See above note 61.

[78] "The Hymn of Praise of the Dge-bshes Lotsāba (i.e. Nag-tsho Tshul-khrims rgyal-ba)".

The *Bstod-pa brgyad-cu-pa* as extant in the Mang-yul Gung-thang xylograph

SIGLA AND SIGNS

A *Jo-bo-rje'i bstod-pa brgyad-cu-pa nag-tsho lo-tstsha-ba tshul-khrims rgyal-bas mdzad pa* (References to folios, pages and lines are given in brackets)

B *Jo-bo-rje'i bstod-pa brgyad-cu-pa nag-tsho lo-tsā bas mdzad pa* as contained on fol. 15b1-20a5 of the *Bang-mdzod*, full title: *Legs-par bshad-pa bka'-gdams rin-po-che'i gsung-gi gces-btus nor-bu'i bang-mdzod* (References to folios, pages and lines are given in parentheses)

G *Bka'-gdams chos-'byung sgron-me*, full title: *Bka'-gdams-kyi rnam-par thar-pa bka'-gdams chos-'byung gsal-ba'i sgron-me*

H *Bka'-gdams chos-'byung rnam-thar*, full title: *Bka'-gdams rin-po-che'i chos-'byung rnam-thar nyin-mor byed-pa'i 'od-stong*

L *Rnam-thar rgyas-pa*, full title: *Jo-bo-rje dpal-ldan mar-me-mdzad ye-shes-kyi rnam-thar rgyas-pa*

P *Lam-sgron rnam-bshad*, full title: *Byang-chub lam-gyi sgron-ma'i rnam-bshad phul-byung bzhad-pa'i dga'-ston*

R *Rnam-thar yongs-grags*, full title: *Jo-bo rin-po-che dpal-ldan a-ti-sha'i rnam-thar rgyas-pa yongs-grags*

T *Lam-rim chen-mo*, full title: *[Skyes-bu gsum-gyi nyams-su blang-ba'i] Rim-pa thams-cad tshang-bar ston-pa'i byang-chub lam-gyi rim pa*

Y *Lam-rnam*, full title: *Byang-chub lam-gyi rim-pa'i bla-ma brgyud-pa'i rnam-par thar-pa rgyal-bstan mdzes-pa'i rgyan mchog-tu phul-byung nor-bu'i phreng-ba*

_ (underlined letter) a subscribed letter (only recorded when occurring in A)
— (hyphen) ample space between letters due to the extinction of a sign (only recorded when occurring in A)
[] (brackets) see A
() (parentheses) see B
⟨⟩ (angle brackets) letters added for explaining abbreviated spellings

The Text

[1a] jo bo rje'i bstod pa brgyad cu pa nag (15b2) tsho lo *tstsha ba tshul khrims rgyal*[1] bas mdzad pa *bzhugs lags so*[2] | |
[1b] na mo gu ru ma ñdzu gho ṣa ya |

lines 1-8 **G** 28b3-4 (de yang paṇḍi ta **sa'i snying pos** bstod pa las | longs spyod phun sum tshogs pa'i che ba'i dbang du byas na); **L** 22b1-3 (paṇḍi ta **sa'i snying pos** rang gi bla ma yongs su spyod phun sum tshogs pa'i sgo nas bstod pa nas kyang)
lines 1-8, lines 10-19, lines 22-23, and lines 20-21 **H** 22a2-5 (paṇḍi ta **sa'i snying pos** rigs phu⟨n su⟩ṃ ⟨tsh⟩ogs par bstod pa las); **T** 3a4-7 (**lo tstsha ba** chen po **nag tshos** mdzad pa'i bstod pa **brgyad cu pa** las); **Y** 175b3-6 (… jo bo'i bstod pa **brgyad cu pa** las)

| shar phyogs za hor yul mchog na |
| de na grong khyer chen po yod |
| bi kra ma *ni pu ra*[3] yin |
| de yi dbus na rgyal po'i khab |
| [2] pho brang shin *du*[4] yangs pa yod |
| gser gyi rgyal mtshan can (3) zhes bya |

1 tsā B.
2 ni B.
3 la pu ri HL, ni pū ra T.
4 tu BGLTY.

| longs spyod *mnga' thang 'byor pa*[5] ni |
| rgya nag stong *khun*[6] rgyal *po*[7] 'dra | [8]

| khyim ni 'bum phrag nyi shu bdun |

lines 10-19, lines 22-23, and lines 20-21 **G** 28b5-29a1 (rigs phun sum tshogs pa'i che ba'i dbang du byas na); **L** 23a1-3 (paṇḍi ta **sa'i snying pos** rang gi bla ma rigs phun sum tshogs pa'i sgo nas bstod pa nas kyang)

| yul de'i rgyal po [3] *dge ba*[9] dpal | [10]
| btsun mo dpal *mo*[11] 'od zer can |
| yab yum gnyis (4) la sras gsum mnga' |
| *padma'i*[12] snying *dang*[13] *zla ba'i snying*[14] |
| dpal gyi snying po zhes bya 'o |
| rgyal *bu*[15] *pa dma'i*[16] snying po la |
| btsun mo [4] lnga yod sras ni dgu |
| sras kyi thu bo bsod nams dpal |
| da lta'i dus na mkhas pa *che*[17] |
| *dha na shrī*[18] zhes *bya bar*[19] grags |
| (5) 'bring po zla ba'i snying po ni |

---

[5] 'byor pa mnga' thang G.

[6] 'khun GL.

[7] pa T.

[8] After this line, B adds in smaller letters: *stong khun ni rgya nag skad de shar rgyal po zer* | .

[9] dge ba'i BGHLT, dag pa'i Y.

[10] L adds the line: *de yi sras ni dga' ba'i dpal* | .

[11] mo'i B.

[12] pad ma'i LT.

[13] po GHL.

[14] zla snying po GL.

[15] po G.

[16] pad ma'i LT.

[17] cha T.

[18] dhā na shrī G, dha na shri L.

[19] by⟨a b⟩ar GL.

| da lta bla ma rje btsun yin |
| chung ba dpal gyi [5] *snying*[20] po ni |
| dge slong *birya*[21] *tsantra*[22] yin |

lines 24-25 **G** 29a5 (**sa'i snying pos**); **L** 27b5-6 (paṇḍi ta **sa'i snying po**'i bstod pa nas)

| *de*[23] lta bu *yi*[24] *bhaṃ ga*[25] la'i |
| rgyal srid spangs nas thar par gshegs |[26]

| khyod ni yon tan kun gyi 'byung gnas te |
| yon tan rgya mtsho ltar zab thugs rje can |
| mkhas [6] pa chen po khyod kyi yon tan las |
| don dang ldan par bdag gis bstod par bgyi |

| (16a) rig pa'i gnas lnga dag gi mkhyen pa rgyas |
| bdag dang gzhan *dag*[27] mnyam pa nyid du mdzad |
| *yang na*[28] bdag gzhan [7] *rje*[29] bar mdzad pa yi |
| dpal ldan mar me mdzad la phyag 'tshal lo |

lines 34-35 **T** 4b3-4 (bstod pa las); **Y** 176a6-b1 (bstod pa las)
lines 34-37 **G** 38b5-6 (bstod pa las); **L** 38b1-2 (dge bshes **lo tsā ba**'i bstod pa nas kyang)

---

20 snying ⟨p⟩o [*sic*] H.

21 bhirya L, biryā T, bīrya Y.

22 tsandra BGLTY.

23 da B.

24 om. L.

25 bhangga G.

26 B adds in smaller letters after this line: *'di yan jo bo'i rigs phun sum tshogs par bstod pa pa ṇḍi ta sa'i snying pos mdzad (6) par bsod nams lha'i dbang po dang las chen gnyis gsungs.*

L adds the line: *a ti sha la phyag 'tshal lo* | | .

27 gyi B.

28 yab ni B.

29 brje B.

| rang don yal bar (2) dor nas gzhan gyi don |
| lhur mdzad de ni bdag gi bla ma *yin*[30] |
| dngos sam brgyud pas *gzhan don rtag tu*[31] [2a] mdzad |
| bla ma snying rje can la phyag 'tshal lo |

lines 38-41 **G** 36b1-2 (de yang bstod par); **L** 41b3-4 (de la **lo tsā ba**'i bstod pa nas); **T** 4a6-7 (bstod pa las)
lines 38-49 **R** 26b3-5 (**lo tsā ba**' i bstod pa las)

| khyod ni nyan thos theg pa'i *sgor*[32] zhugs nas |
| tshul khrims g.yag (3) rnga bzhin du *bsrung*[33] mdzad *cing*[34] |
| tshangs spyod dpal dang ldan pa'i dge slong *mchog*[35]
| gnas brtan 'dul ba 'dzin la phyag 'tshal lo |

lines 42-45 **G** 36b4 (… zhes so); **L** 42a1 (**lo tsā ba**'i bstod pa nas); **T** 4b1-2 (bstod pa las)

| khyod ni [2] pha rol phyin pa'i sgor zhugs nas |
| lhag pa'i bsam pa rnam par dag *pa yi*[36] |
| byang chub (4) *sems kyis*[37] 'gro rnams mi gtong *ba'i*[38] |
| blo ldan snying rje can la phyag 'tshal lo |

lines 46-49 **G** 36b6-37a1 (spyir bstod pa yin te); **L** 42a3-4 (**lo tsā ba**'i bstod pa nas); **T** 4b6-7 (bstod pa las)

| khyod ni *gsang sngags*[39] theg pa'i *sgor*[40] zhugs nas |
| *rang lhar gzigs shing*[41] rdo rje'i thugs dang ldan |

---

30 lags BGLTY.
31 rtag tu gzhan don GL.
32 skor T.
33 srung T.
34 pa'i B.
35 mdzad LR.
36 gyur cing GLT, gyur te R.
37 thugs kyis T, sems kyi G.
38 ba GLT.
39 rdo rje T.
40 skor T.
41 rang lus lhar gzigs G.

| rnal [3] 'byor dbang phyug a *va bhū ti*[42] pa |
| sbas (5) pa'i brtul *shugs 'dzin*[43] la phyag 'tshal lo |

lines 50-53 **G** 29a1-2 (**lo tstsha ba**'i bstod pa **brgyad cu pa** las kyang); **P** 2a3 (**lo tstsha** bas)

| rigs kyi nang nas mchog gyur pa |
| khyod ni rgyal po'i rigs su 'khrungs |
| dregs pas myos pa thams cad kyang |
| zhabs kyi *padmar*[44] spyi bos gtugs |

lines 54-57 **G** 29a5-6 (**lo tstsha bas** … ces bstod pa ltar ro)

| 'khor ba'i skyon dang mtshang [4] (6) gzigs pas |
| *bhaṃ ga*[45] la yi rgyal srid de |
| mchil ma'i thal ba bzhin bor nas |
| sangs rgyas bstan pa rgyas par mdzad |

lines 58-67 **G** 41a4-5 (bstod pa las)
lines 58-70 **L** 40b5-6 (de la **lo tsā ba**'i bstod pa nas); **H** 25a2-4 (shes dang | …); **T** 5b2-4 (ces dang | …)
lines 64-67 **P** 3b1 (following line 250)
lines 68-70 **G** 41b1-2 (bstod pa las)

| o *tanta yi pu*[46] ri na |
| *rab byung*[47] brgya phrag phyed dang gsum |
| *bhri kā ma ni*[48] shī la na |
| rab byung brgya phrag *ma longs* (16b) *tsam*[49] |
| rtsa ba'i sde bzhi tshang bar *bzhugs*[50] | [5]

---

42 va dhu tī B, ba dhu tī T, ba dhū tī GL, va dhū ti R.
43 zhugs 'dzin B, zhugs mdzad GLRT.
44 padmor B.
45 bhangga BG.
46 tan ta yi pu L, tan ta yi pū T.
47 rab tu byung ba L.
48 bi kra ma ni B, bi ka ma ni GL, bi kra ma la HT.
49 ma long tsam L, mang po dang H.
50 zhugs B.

| sde pa'i *khyed grags*[51] *khyod mi mdzad*[52] |
| ma ga *dhā*[53] yi yul gyi ni |
| gnas gzhi *ma lus*[54] thams cad kyi |
| ston pa'i 'khor ni bzhi po yi |
| kun gyi gtsug gi nor bur gyur |
| khyod ni sde pa *bco*[55] brgyad (2) kyi |
| kun gyi spyi la bzhugs pas na |
| thams cad kyis ni lung yang len |

lines 71-74 **G** 33b4 (... ces pa dang)

| khyod kyis [6] 'jig rten chos brgyad po |
| thaṃs cad khyad ⟨d⟩u bsad nas ni |
| gzhan dag ji ltar mos pa yi |
| sems dang *stun*[56] pa'i spyod *lam*[57] mdzad |

lines 75-80 **G** 52b3-4 (de yang bstod pa las)
lines 81-82 **G** 54a2 (bstod pa las kyang)

| gzhan (3) dag dad par mi 'gyur zhing |
| mi rnams sems dang 'gal gyur pa |
| gshe zhing *bskur*[58] ba 'debs la sogs |
| gzhan gyi [7] sdig rkyen khyod mi mdzad |

| nam yang gzhan dag mi dad pa |
| dug dang 'dra *bar*[59] spong bar mdzad |
| slob ma ji ltar (4) 'dod pa yi |
| chos kyi gdams ngag *gsung bar*[60] mdzad |

---

51 khengs dregs BGHT, kheng grags L.
52 mi mdzad pas G, mi mdzad de H.
53 dha BGHLPT.
54 m⟨a l⟩us H.
55 bcva H.
56 bstun BG.
57 pa BG.
58 skur BG.
59 ste G.
60 gsungs par B.

lines 83-86 **G** 33b3 (… zhes so)

| 'jig rten mi rnams thams cad kyis |
| brnyas shing *bskur*[61] ba 'debs pa dang |
| phrag dog rngan *can*[62] byed [2b] na yang |
| gnyen po *mdzad*[63] nas phyir la 'gyes |

lines 87-90 **G** 29a6-b1 (**lo tstsha bas**)
lines 87 and 90 **L** 13a4-5 (**lo tsā ba**'i bstod pa nas)

| khyod *kyi*[64] sku lus (5) mthong *ba na*[65] |
| thams cad *'thun*[66] par shin *du*[67] mos |
| sku *mdangs*[68] 'jam zhing gsal *ba dang*[69] |
| dang po tha ma'i mig chags 'gyur |[70]

lines 91-94 **G** 29b2 (… ces pa ltar ro)

| rnam par 'tshe ba spangs pa *yin*[71] |
| khyod kyi sku la snyun mi mnga' |
| bsod nams tshogs [2] ni bsags (6) pa yis |
| zhal mthong tsam gyis dad *pa*[72] byed |[73]

---

61 skur BG.
62 chen G.
63 bsten BG.
64 nyid L.
65 ba'i 'dun L.
66 mthun BG.
67 tu B.
68 mdog G.
69 bas na G.
70 L adds:
| *tshogs ni bsags pa dag gi rgyus* |
| *zhabs la 'khor lo'i mtshan gyis brgyan* | .
71 yis BG.
72 par G.
73 This line is missing in A.

lines 95-98 **G** 29b3 (... zhes pa ltar ro)

| khyod ni spyod lam thams cad du |
| chos dang *'thun*[74] par mdzad pa yis |
| 'jig rten kha na ma tho ba |
| grags pa ngan pas khyod mi gos |

lines 99-102 **G** 34a2 (... ces so)

| tshul khrims rnam par dag gyur pas |
| skyob pa (17a) shā kya *seng ge de'i*[75] |
| zab pa dang ni rgya che ba'i |
| bstan pa khyod kyi thugs [3] la gnas |

lines 103-106 **G** 42a5 (bstod pa las)

| sangs rgyas bstan pa rin po che |
| *bsrung*[76] dang *'dzen*[77] dang skyong ba *yin*[78] |
| 'dren pa khyod ni 'das pa na |
| bstan pa *rol du*[79] nub *pa* (2) *yin*[80] |

| mtho dang dma' dang mnyam pa la |
| phrag dog rngan can 'gran mi mnga' |
| de ltar khyod ni thams cad kyis |
| gtso bo bzhin du [4] bkur ba yin |

lines 111-112 **G** 30a5 (bstod pa las kyang)
lines 111-114 **L** 23b4 (dge bshes **lo tsā ba**'i bstod pa nas kyang); **T** 3a8-b1 (bstod pa las)
lines 115-116 **G** 30a5 (... zhes gsungs so)

---

74 mthun BG.
75 sengge yi B, sengge de'i G.
76 bskur B, srung G.
77 'dzin BG.
78 yi BG.
79 phal cher G.
80 dang 'dra BG.

| lo *ni*[81] nyi shu rtsa gcig na |
| *sgyu*[82] rtsal drug *bcu*[83] rtsa bzhi dang |
| *gzo*[84] yi gnas *ni*[85] thams (3) cad dang |
| legs par sbyar ba'i skad dang ni |
| sgra yi— bstan bcos thams cad dang |
| tshad ma kun la mkhas pa *yin*[86] |

lines 117-120 **G** 32a5 (bstod pa las)
lines 119-122 **P** 2b6-3a1 (bstod pa las)

| bla ma bzang po mang bsten pas̲ |
| khyod ni thos̲ pa'̲i rgyan *gyis*[87] [5] brgyan |
| theg pa gsuṃ[88] dang sde snod gsuṃ |
| khyod ni mkhas̲ (4) pa chen po yin̲ |

lines 121-124 **G** 42a3-4 (bstod pa las kyang)

| khyod ni mkhas pa mang po *yi*[89] |
| brda la bdar ba'i skyes bu yin |
| bdag dang gzhan *gyi*[90] rgol ba ni |
| kun kyang tshar bcad phan par mdzad |

lines 127-128 **G** 32a1 (… zhes 'byung ba ltar ro); **L** 28a3 (**lo tsā ba**'i bstod pa nas kyang); **T** 3b7 (bstod pa las)

---

81 na B.
82 rgyu L.
83 cu BGLT.
84 bzo BLT.
85 na B.
86 lags BGLT.
87 gyi BG.
88 Up to the end of line 121 squeezed letters in A.
89 yis GP.
90 gyis G.

| sangs rgyas ye shes zhal *mnga'* [91] *ba'i*[92] |
| slob ma brgyud *pa*[93] brgyud du 'khrungs | [6]
| khyod kyi (5) mkhan po sbyor lam pa |
| yin par kun la *rab tu grags*[94] |

lines 129-131 **R** 20b3 (... **lo tsā ba**'i bstod pa las)
lines 129-136 **G** 32b1-2 (... zhes gsungs so); **L** 10a4-5 (**lo tsā ba**'i bstod pa nas); **H** 23a5-6 (**lo tsā ba**'i bstod pa las); **T** 6b3-4 (bstod pa las)

| *rtag tu*[95] bsten pa'i bla ma ni |
| *shanti pa dang gser gling pa*[96] |
| *bha tra bo dhi dznyā na shrī*[97] |
| dngos grub thob pa mang po dang |
| khyad par du *yang*[98] klu sgrub nas |
| gcig nas gcig tu brgyud pa (6) yi |
| zab pa dang ni rgya che ba'i | [7]
| gdams pa *khyod*[99] la mnga' ba *yin*[100] |

lines 137-138 **G** 37a6 (bstod pa las kyang)
line 139 **G** 41b4 (... zhes dang)
lines 139-142 **G** 36b2 (... zhes gsungs so)

| khyod ni sangs rgyas thams cad kyi |
| byin *brlabs thugs las skyes pa*[101] yin |
| khyod ni bslab pa gsum ldan pas |

---

91 Illegible in B.

92 yi B.

93 pa'i B.

94 grags pa lags BG, grags pa yin L.

95 yun ring G.

96 sha nti dang gser gling pa B, shānti dang gser gling pa HT, gser gling pa dang shanti pa R.

97 bha dra bo dhi dznyā na shrī BGLT, byang chub bzang po dze ta ri R.

98 ni HT.

99 khyed H.

100 lags G.

101 rlabs thugs la skye ba B, rlabs thugs la skyes pa G.

| chal ba'i *tshul khrims bsal*[102] ba yin |
| tshul (17b) khrims dri *ngad*[103] ldan pas na |
| ring na gnas pa rnams kyang [3a] 'du |

lines 143-148 **G** 33b1-2 (… zhes gsungs so)
lines 145-146 **P** 3a2-3 (bstod pa las)
lines 145-148 **L** 42b2-3 (dge bshes **lo tsā ba**'i bstod pa nas); **T** 4b8-5a1 (bstod pa las); **Y** 176b4-5 (bstod pa las)
lines 147-148 **G** 37a1 (… zhes gsungs par ltar ro)

| kha na ma tho phra rab la'ang |
| thugs ni shin *du*[104] 'jigs par mdzad |
| dran dang shes bzhin ldan pa yis |
| tshul *khrims*[105] ma yin yid mi mdzad |
| bag yod dran *pas*[106] g.yo *sgyu*[107] (2) med |
| ltung ba'i nyes pas khyod ma gos |

lines 149-152 **G** 33a7-b1 (… ces so)

| 'di la mi sbyin di la sbyin |
| 'di [2] *la—*[108] mi *dbul 'di la dbul*[109] |
| thugs ni *kun*[110] la snyoms gyur pas |
| gang la'ang bye brag *'byer*[111] mi mdzad | [112]

---

102 dri ma gsal G.

103 dang G.

104 tu BG.

105 bzhin BGLP.

106 dang BGLTY.

107 rgyu L.

108 la BG.

109 'bul 'di la 'bul BG.

110 rkun (?) G.

111 dbyer BG.

112 Lines 149-152 are also given in the eulogy on Atiśa by Lha bla-ma Byang-chub-'od (Mang-yul Gung-thang print, fol 5b1) in the following form:
| *thugs ni shin du snyoms gyur pas* |
| *'di la mi sbyin 'di la sbyin* |
| *'di la mi dbul 'di la dbul* |
| *gang la'ang bye brag 'byed mi mdzad* | .

lines 153-156 **G** 54b4-5 (bstod pa las kyang); **L** 3a2 (da (for: de) la **lo tsā ba**'i bstod pa nas)

| dkon *mchog*[113] gsum dang thugs dam lha |
| bla ma rnams (3) dang 'gro ba lnga |
| 'di drug nga yi lha dang ni |
| jo bo yin zhes rtag tu *gsungs*[114] |[115]

lines 157-158 **G** 33b7-34a1 (... zhes gsungs so)
lines 157 and 176 **P** 3a5 (bstod pa las)
lines 159-160 **G** 34a1-2 (... ces so)

| khyod ni stong nyid rnal 'byor pa |
| rtag [3] tu chos sku'i ngang la gnas |
| gzugs sku *nyid kyis*[116] thugs dam lha |
| thun *'tshams*[117] rnal 'byor *yengs mi mnga'*[118] |

lines 161-168 **G** 37b2-3 (bstod pa las); **T** 6a7-b1 (bstod pa las)
lines 161-163 and 165-168 **L** 2b5-6 (**lo tsā ba**'i bstod pa **brgyad cu pa** nas kyang)

| dpal (4) ldan *dgyes pa'i*[119] rdo rje dang |
| dam tshig *bkod pa'i*[120] rgyal po dang |
| dpa' bo *'jig rten*[121] dbang phyug dang |
| jo mo rje btsun sgrol ma sogs |

---

[113] cog GL.

[114] gsung GL.

[115] Lines 153-156 are also given after the parallel to lines 149-152 in the eulogy on Atiśa by Lha bla-ma Byang-chub-'od (Mang-yul Gung-thang print, fol 5b1-2) in the following form:

| *rang gi lha dang bla ma dang* |
| *dkon mchog gsum dang 'gro ba lnga* |
| *'di drug nga yi lha dang ni* |
| *jo bo yin zhes [2] rtag tu gsung* |

[116] gnyis kyi G, nyid kyi B.

[117] mtshams B.

[118] yengs mi mdzad BG.

[119] dgyes pa G, bgyes pa L.

[120] gsum bkod G.

[121] lo ka L.

| zhal [4] gzigs *gnang*[122] ba thob *pa dang*[123] |
| rmi lam na 'am mngon sum du |
| zab pa dang ni rgya che ba'i |
| dam (5) chos rtag tu gsan pa *yin*[124] |

lines 169-170 **P** 3a3-4 (bstod par)
lines 169 and 172 **T** 5a6-7 (bstod pa las)
lines 169-174 **G** 31a4-5 (… ces so)

| gsang sngags theg pa'i gzhung ltar na |
| *skyed*[125] pa'i rim pa brtan par nges |
| pha rol phyin pa'i gzhung ltar na |
| sbyor ba'i lam pa yin par̲ gsal | [5]

lines 175-176 **G** 31a6 (… zhes gsungs pa ltar); **G** 41b4 (… zhes bshad pa ltar)

| rang lhar̲ byin gyis̲ brlabs so zhes |
| grags *pa*[126] snyan (6) *pa*[127] phyogs bcur *gda'*[128] |
| khyod ni gsang sngags rnal 'byor pa |
| dri med rdo *rje'i*[129] thugs̲ dang ldan |

lines 177-186 **G** 47b2-3 (bstod pa las kyang); **L** 69a5-b1 (de la **lo tstsha ba**'i bstod nas kyang); **R** 59a1-2 (**lo tsā ba**'i bstod pa las)
lines 177-188 **G** 91a4-6 (… zhes gsungs pa ltar ro); **Y** 200a3-5 (… zhes gsungs pa ltar ro)

| khyod *sngon*[130] so ma pu ri na |
| rtog ge 'bar ba *gsung ba'i*[131] tshe |

---

122 In G only the closing *ng* is legible.
123 pas na BGT, pa na L.
124 lags BGLT.
125 bskyed BGL.
126 pa'i G.
127 pas BG.
128 khyab BG.
129 rje B.
130 ni R.
131 gsungs pa'i B.

| da ni lo ni nyi shu *na*[132] |
| tshe yi 'du byed gtong *'gyur gsung*[133] |
| de nas lo [6] *gnyis* (18a) *lon pa na*[134] |
| bod du *byon*[135] *ka'i*[136] dus su ni |
| *bhi kā*[137] ma *ni*[138] *shī*[139] *la na*[140] |
| da ni lo ni bco brgyad na |
| tshe yi 'du byed btang nas *su*[141] |
| lus *'di*[142] bod du 'jog go *gsung*[143] |
| ji skad *gsung*[144] bzhin ma 'khrul par |
| *byung ba*[145] de ni ngo mtshar (2) che |

lines 189-197 **G** 63a2-4 (bstod pa las)

| khyod kyi rnam smin sku lus de |
| bod kyi yul [7] du *bzhags*[146] nas su |
| smon lam *gyi*[147] ni sku lus de |
| byams pa'i spyan sngar dga' ldan du |
| 'khrungs par sgrol mas lung bstan *gsung*[148] |

---

132 nas R.
133 zhes gsungs Y.
134 ni lon pa na B, ni gnyis na ni L.
135 'byon BGY.
136 kha'i GY.
137 bi kra BG, bri ka L, bi ka Y.
138 la BGRY, la ni (*ni* is added below the line) L.
139 shi R.
140 lar ni BGY.
141 ni BG, su G 91a5, om. L.
142 ni LR.
143 gsungs Y.
144 gsungs BG.
145 gyur pa G.
146 bzhag BG.
147 gyis BG.
148 gsungs B.

| nam mkha' dri med ces bya ba'i |
| lha yi bur ni 'khrungs (3) par 'gyur |
| zab pa dang ni rgya che ba'i |
| chos ni byams *pa'i*[149] mgon *la*[150] gsan | [3b]

lines 198-201 **G** 42b6-43a1 (**brgyad cu pa** las)

| des na khyod ni 'dzam gling gi |
| rgyan du gyur pa chen po yin |
| snyan par grags shing 'gran zla med |
| mkhas pa rnams kyi bla mar 'os |

lines 202-209 **G** 30b5-6 (de skad du yang)

| dpal ldan rdo rje sems (4) dpa' yis |
| gsungs pa'i gsang sngags rgyud sde *yi*[151] |
| rim pa gnyis *pa'i*[152] man ngag ni |
| mkhas pa mang po'i [2] brgyud pa mnga' |

| gsang sngags phyi nang rgyud sde dang |
| mkhas pa mang pos mdzad pa'i gzhung |
| gzigs dang gsan dang bshad (5) pa yis |
| gzhung la shin *du gams*[153] par mdzad |

lines 210-217 **G** 62b4-5 (bstod pa las kyang)

| khyod kyis slob ma'i tshogs la ni |
| gdams ngag rtsa bar *gsung ba*[154] ni |
| bsags pa'i yo [3] byad thams cad *ni*[155] |
| 'khor ba'i rgyur ni ma *btang gsung*[156] |

---

[149] pa G.

[150] las B.

[151] bzhi BG.

[152] kyi G.

[153] tu goms BG.

[154] gsungs pa BG.

[155] kyang G.

[156] btang gsungs B, gtang gsungs G.

| gzhan *gyi*[157] brnyas thabs byas pa (6) *dang*[158] |
| glo bur nyon mongs skyes pa dang |
| gzhan dang rtsod pa byung *nas*[159] yang |
| *gnyan*[160] pos myur du zlog cig *gsung*[161] |

lines 218-219 **G** 29b4 (bstod pa las kyang)
lines 220-221 **G** 29b6 (bstod pa las kyang)

| sngon gyi sbyin pa'i 'bras bu yis |
| gzhan gyis bsags pa khyod [4] la 'bul |
| yo byad mnga' ba thams cad kyang |
| longs (18b) spyod bsrung *phyir*[162] chud mi *gson*[163] |

lines 222-225 **G** 30a1 (... ces so)

| dge ba mdzad pa thams cad kyang |
| 'khor ba'i rgyu ni *spangs pa'i*[164] phyir |
| 'khor gsum yongs su dag pa dang |
| stong pas ma zin gang yang med |

lines 226-231 **G** 51a4-5 (bstod pa las kyang)
lines 232-233 **G** 58b4 (bstod pa las)

| dge ba'i bshes gnyen dang [5] bral zhing |
| theg chen mdo sde ma *thes* (2) *pas*[165] |
| snying rje las byung byang chub sems |
| spangs nas gsang sngags 'ba' zhig spyod |

---

157 gyis BG.
158 kyang G.
159 na G.
160 gnyen BG.
161 gsungs BG.
162 zhing G.
163 gzon BG.
164 spang ba'i BG.
165 thos pas B, mthong bas G.

| gnod sbyin lag na rdo rje dang |
| srin *bu*[166] sha za sogs par skye |
| khyod *kyi*[167] shes rab thugs rje yis |
| shing rta chen po'i lam du btsud |

lines 234-237 **G** 51a5 (... ces 'byung ngo)

| [6] rgyud kyi dgongs (3) pa *sgra gzhin pa*[?][168] |
| *'dzin pa'i sngags pa kun la ni*[169] |
| log pa'i lam du zhugs *gzigs*[170] nas |
| khyod kyis yang dag lam du btsud |

lines 238-245 **G** 51b3-4 (bstod pa las)
lines 238-241 **G** 34a3 (... zhes so)

| lta ba mi mthun sna tshogs pa |
| sngon gyi slob dpon rjes 'brangs nas |
| so sor mi mthun rtsod pa kun |
| (4) khyod *kyi*[171] lung dang [7] *rigs*[172] pas bkrol |

| khyod ni sangs rgyas bstan pa yi |
| kha 'byed nyi *ma chen po*[173] yin |
| phyin ci log gi lta 'dzin pa |
| khyod kyis yang dag *bstan*[174] la btsud |

lines 246-251 **G** 40b5-6 (don 'di yang **brgyad cu pa** las); **H** 25a1-2 (**lo tsā ba**'i bstod pa las); **L** 18b6-19a1 (dge bshes **lo tsā ba**'i bstod pa nas); **T** 5b1-2 (bstod pa las)
lines 247-250 **P** 3a7 (bstod pa las)
lines 248-251 **L** 10a1-2 (**lo tsā ba**'i bstod pa nas)

---

166 po BG.
167 nyid G.
168 mi shes par BG.
169 sgra bzhin 'jug pa'i sngags pa kun BG.
170 zin G.
171 kyis BG.
172 rig BG.
173 ma'i 'od zer BG.
174 lam G.

| byang chub chen po'i pho brang du |
| thams cad 'dus shing *'tshogs*[175] (5) pa *na*[176] |
| rang dang gzhan gyi sde pa yi |
| grub mtha' [4a] ngan pa'i rgol ba kun |
| seng *ge*[177] nga ro'i sgra skad kyis |
| thams cad kyi *ni*[178] klad pa 'gems |

lines 252-253 **G** 33b5 (... ces so)
lines 254-255 **G** 33b6 (... ces so)

| chos kyi dbyings na rtag bzhugs pas |
| ye shes tshogs ni *rdzogs*[179] par mdzad |
| theg chen mdo sde (6) las gsungs pa'i |
| thabs kyis bsod nams tshogs *bsags*[180] [2] mdzad |

| khyad par can gyi bsod nams tshogs |
| myur du rdzogs par mdzad pa'i phyir |
| gsang sngags rgyud sde thabs *kyi*[181] ni |
| 'bad pa med par rdzogs par mdzad |

lines 260-263 **G** 56b2 (bstod pa las kyang); **L** 38a5 (dge bshes **lo tsā ba**'i bstod pa nas kyang)

| khyod (19a) ni *mthong*[182] dang *thos pa*[183] dang |
| reg par gyur *na*[184] thams cad *kyis*[185] |

---

175 tshogs P.
176 las L.
177 ge'i GLHT.
178 om. L 10a2.
179 gsog G.
180 rdzogs G.
181 kyis B.
182 thos G.
183 mthong ba G.
184 pa BG, nas L.
185 kyang L.

| *mos*[186] *cing*[187] bsnyen bkur byed la *brtson*[188] |
| khyod 'dra [3] 'dzam *bu*[189] gling na *dkon*[190] |

lines 264-267 **G** 33a4-5 (... ces pa ltar ro)

| khyod ni sku na *sgres*[191] na yang |
| lhag pa'i bsam pa rnam dag pas |
| (2) gzhan don gtso bor mdzad pa'i phyir |
| lo *zla shul*[192] yang *sgrod*[193] par mdzad |

lines 268-271 **L** 37b1-2 (dge bshes **lo tsā ba**'i bstod pa nas);
R 25b4-6 (**lo tsā ba**'i bstod pa las kyang)
lines 268-275 **G** 33a2-4 (... zhes pa ltar ro)

| sems can *sdug bsngal*[194] can gzigs *na*[195] |
| thugs kyis *mi*[196] bzod spyan chab *'byung*[197] |
| snying rjes thugs ni gdungs [4] pa khyod |
| rtag tu gzhan don 'ba' zhig mdzad |

| (3) des na khyod la thams cad kyis |
| bsnyen bkur chen po bya bar rigs |
| gang zag dam pa khyod lta bu |
| yul phyogs gang na'ang yod ma yin |

---

186 dad BG.
187 shing L.
188 sogs L.
189 bu'i GL.
190 med L.
191 bgres BG.
192 zla'i bshul G.
193 bgrod BG.
194 duḥ kha L.
195 nas G.
196 ma L.
197 byung B.

lines 276-292 **G** 39a3-5 (... ces gsungs so); **L** 36b1-4 (dge bshes **lo tsā ba**'i bstod pa nas); **R** 32b4-6 (**lo tsā ba**'i bstod pa las); **Y** 160a2 (bstod pa las)

| rgyal po *ne ya pa*[198] la dang |
| nub phyogs *karna'i*[199] rgyal po gnyis |
| rtsod pa chen po byung ba'i [5] tshe |
| nub (4) phyogs *karna'i*[200] rgyal po yis |
| ma ga dhar ni dmag drangs pas |
| grong khyer ma thub gnas gzhir drangs |
| rab byung dge bsnyen lnga yang bsad |
| yo byad mang po *gnang* ⟨*s*⟩*u*[201] khyer |
| *khyed*[202] la zhe sdang mi mnga' bas |
| *rko*[203] long *ma*[204] mdzad snying rje 'khrungs |
| (5) g.yul *log*[205] tshe na dmag *mi'i* [6] *skyabs*[206] |
| *byas*[207] nas bla mas *sdum*[208] mdzad *pas*[209] |
| 'tsho ba'i yo byad ma gtogs *pa'i*[210] |
| yo byad lhag ma med par btang |
| lus dang srog la ma gzigs par |
| chu bo chen po yang yang *rgal*[211] |
| de gnyis *sdums*[212] (6) nas mdza' bor mdzad |

---

198 nairya pha B, nairya pā GY, ne ya pā LR.
199 karṇa'i BGLRY.
200 karṇa'i BGLRY.
201 nang du B, gnang du GY.
202 khyod BGLY.
203 ko BGLRY.
204 mi R.
205 bzlog L.
206 mi bskyabs GLRY.
207 phyi GLRY.
208 bsdum B, bsdums G, sdums L, 'dums Y.
209 de BGLRY.
210 pa BGY.
211 brgal BGLRY.
212 bsdums BG, bzlum L, 'dums Y, sdun R.

lines 295-302 **G** 33a5-6 (… zhes pa ltar ro)

| snying rjes sems can mi gtong bas |
| thub [7] pa'i brtul *shugs*[213] khyod kyis bsrungs |
| khyod la bdag dang gzhan med pas |
| dgra *zin 'pham la*[214] khengs *grags*[215] med |

| kun gyi pha ma khyod lta bu |
| *ding*[216] sang— dus na ngo (19b) mtshar che |

| rgyu 'bras 'brel pa chud *gson*[217] pa'i |
| gzhan dag sdig pa byed gzigs *na*[218] |
| *'di ni*[219] 'gro ba [4b] cir 'gyur zhes |
| thugs kyis mi bzod spyan chab 'byung |

| yon tan *sngags*[220] pa mtha' yas pas |
| phyogs bcur grags (2) pa snyan pas khyab |

| bdag gi gdung ba *bsel*[221] ba'i phyir |
| bla ma rje btsun la bstod pa |
| bdag gis bstod par ma zad kyi |
| gang zag gzhan rnams khyod la [2] bstod |

lines 309-310 **G** 33b4-5 (… ces gsuns pa ltar ro)

| bstod pa dang ni smad pa yis |
| khyod la *dges dang mi dges*[222] med |

---

213 zhugs B.
214 zun pham la B, zun pham rgyal G.
215 dregs BG.
216 deng B.
217 gzon BG.
218 pa G.
219 de yi G.
220 bsngags B.
221 sel B.
222 dgyes dang mi dgyes G.

| yon (3) tan rgya mtsho khyod bstod pas |
| bdag gi yid ni shin tu *tshim*[223] |
| khyod mthong nas ni dad gyur nas |
| kun kyang bsnyen bkur byed la brtson |

lines 315-318 **G** 33a2 (... ces pa ltar ro)

| khyod ni gzhan la phan pa dang |
| bde mdzad thugs ni *byung*[224] [3] gyur pas |
| gzhan gyis ji ltar zhus pa (4) bzhin |
| mi gnang *ba*[225] ni khyod mi mdzad |

lines 319-322 **G** 57a1-2 (bstod pa las); **P** 3b4 (bstod pa las); **R** 87b5-6 (**lo tsā ba**'i bstod pa las)

| *bla ma*[226] bod du ma byon na |
| thams cad *long*[227] ba bzhin du 'gyur |
| mkhyen *pas brgyan*[228] pa khyod byon *nas*[229] |
| bod du ye shes nyi ma shar |

lines 323-324 and 326-328 **G** 59b2 (bstod pa las)

| bod du byon *pas*[230] 'brom ston dang |
| khu ston rngog ston la sogs *pa'i*[231] |
| [4] (5) khyod la dad cing 'dun pa yi |
| slob ma'i tshogs ni ma lus pa |
| thams cad ji ltar 'dod pa bzhin |
| kun gyi yid ni *tshim*[232] par mdzad |

---

223 chim B.

224 chung BG.

225 bar BG.

226 jo bo P.

227 leng P.

228 pa rgyas BGR.

229 pas BGR.

230 nas G.

231 pa BG.

232 chim B.

lines 329-330 **G** 60b2 (bstod pa las)
lines 331-332 **G** 58b4 (... ces dang)

| khyod *la*[233] chos 'brel slob *na*[234] ni |
| chud ni za bar mi 'gyur te |
| skyes bu chen po'i chos lugs slob | [235]
| (6) shing rta chen po'i lam du 'dzud |

lines 333-336 **G** 60b1 (**brgyad cu pa** las); **R** 84a3-4[236] (**lo tsā ba**'i bstod pa las)
line 334 **G** 50b4-5 (... zhes so)
lines 334 and 336 **L** 42a4-5 (khong[237] gi zhal nas)

| bla ma dge ba'i bshes gnyen dam pa *khyod*[238] |
| lo [5] ni bcu *dgur*[239] *bsten cing 'grogs na yang*[240] |
| khyod kyi sku gsung thugs la 'khrul pa yi |
| nyes pa'i dri ma byung ba *mthang*[241] re *rkan*[242] |

lines 337-344 **G** 55b6-56a1 (bstod pa las)

| ma ga *dhā*[243] yi bdag po ni |
| rgyal po (20a) *ne ya pa*[244] la yin |
| longs spyod 'byor pa mnga' thang sogs |
| 'di tsam zhes ni brjod par dka' |

---

[233] dang G.
[234] ma G.
[235] This line is missing in A.
[236] This is the seven-syllable version of the stanza, cf. para. 3.3, note 49.
[237] I.e. the Dge bshes Lo tsā ba.
[238] khyed R.
[239] dgu GLR.
[240] brten pa la L [seven syllables only !].
[241] mtheng B, mthong R.
[242] skan BGLR.
[243] dha BG.
[244] nairya phā B, nairya pā G.

| dmag dpung [6] 'bum phrag mang por ldan |
| rab brtan sa *srungs*[245] bu lta *bu*[246] |
| *grags*[247] pas *rnangs zhing*[248] 'gying ba yang |
| khyod kyi zhabs (2) gnyis spyi bor len |

lines 345-348 **G** 56a3-4 (**brgyad cu pa** las)

| gzi brjid ldan pa'i lha rnams dang |
| mthu dang rdzu 'phrul stobs ldan pa'i |
| gnod sbyin tshogs *rnams*[249] ma lus *pa*[250] |
| bsrung zhing bsnyen [7] bkur byed la brtson |

lines 349-352 **G** 65b4-5 (ces gsungs so)

| khyod kyi yon tan dran *pas*[251] na |
| mchi ma *bskru*[252] zhing ba spu ldang |
| bla ma (3) rje btsun khyod dang ni |
| dga' ldan gnas su 'grogs par shog

| nag tsho dge slong tshul khrims rgyal ba yis |
| rang gi bla ma rje btsun bstod pa *yis* |
| rang gi bu la byams pa'i 'gro [5a] ba lnga |
| thams cad dga' ldan gnas su 'grogs par (4) shog

lines 361-363 **G** 65b4 (dge shes **lo tstsha ba**'i zhal nas)

| tshigs bcad brgyad cu *tham—*[253] pa yis |
| bla ma rje btsun bstod pa yis |
| slob ma gnyis slob gsum slob sogs |

---

245 srung G.
246 bur B.
247 dregs BG.
248 rngams shing B, rngams zhing G.
249 ni G.
250 pas G.
251 pa G.
252 dkru B, dk[r]u G.
253 thams B.

| khyod la *dad*[254] cing 'dun pa rnams |
| *shin*[255] *du*[256] dad pa'i yid kyis *su*[257] |
| [2] rtag tu *bstod*[258] pa *gyis*[259] shig ces |
| tshul khrims (5) rgyal *ba—*[260] gsol ba 'debs | |

ces khams gsum chos kyi rgyal po | [261] dpal ldan mar me mdzad ye shes la bstod pa'i rab tu byed pa | [262] *tshig rkang*[263] brgyad cu pa *zhes bya ba*[264] | [265]
nag tsho lo tstsha ba tshul rgyal *bas̱*[266] sbyar ba rdzogs *sho*[267] | | [3]

[appended texts, fol. 5a3-6a7][268]

e ma ho
| rje btsun bla ma chen po'i zhal mnga' nas |
| lho bal yul nas bod kyi yul du byon |
| shul thag ring bas shin du sku nyon mongs |
| 'du ba rnam bzhi'i sku snyun mi mnga 'am |
| sku nyams bde 'am dgyes par byon lags sam |
| sku gsung thugs la gnod pa mi [4] mnga 'am |
| bdag cag bod kyi skye bo phal cher ni |

---

[254] bstod B.
[255] | bla ma'i 'dra 'bag spyan snga ru | | shin G, cf. para. 7.1, note 74.
[256] tu BG.
[257] ni BG.
[258] mchod G.
[259] bgyis B.
[260] bas BG.
[261] om. shad B.
[262] om. shad B.
[263] tshigs bcad B.
[264] 'di B.
[265] | | B.
[266] bas B.
[267] so B.
[268] See above para 2.5, note 35.

| bla ma dang bral bar dgar smra ba de |
| kla klo'i spyod pa ma bsrungs rtsings pas na |
| a ti sha yis bzod par mdzad du gsol |
| slob dpon tshul khrims rgyal ba'i spyan snga nas |
| re ba che bas bdag gis thugs dam zhus | [5]
| thugs la btags nas lho bal yul du byon |
| dka' ba mang pos spyad pa— bzod par zhu |

e ma ho |
| dge slong byang chub 'od bdag gis |
| rtag tu bsams pa'i bla ma spyan drangs pas |
| bod kyi yul du skyes bu mchog 'di yi |
| gzhung lugs shin du dar zhing rgyas par [6] shog |
| za hor rgyal po'i rgyud du sku 'khrungs pa |
| mtshan ni mar me mdzad dpal ye shes zhabs |
| skyes bu 'di yis bla ma mang du bsten |
| snying rje rgyud rlan rin pa'i gnas lnga mkhyen |
| rgol ba tshar bcad mkhas pa chen por grags |
| sdom pa gsum ldan 'bad rtsol drag [7] po yis |
| rang lha'i zhal gzigs rtag tu gzhan don mdzad |
| rdo rje'i sems ldan a va dhū ti pa |
| tshul khrims gy.ag rnga bzhin du bsrung bar mdzad |
| sems can mi gtong byang chub sems stobs ldan |
| bdag dge gzhan gyi sdug bsngal rje mdzad pa'i |
| mar me mdzad dpal [5b] ye shes zhabs phyag 'tshal |
| thugs ni shin du snyoms gyur pas |
| 'di la mi sbyin 'di la sbyin |
| 'di la mi dbul 'di la dbul |
| gang la'ang bye brag 'byed mi mdzad |[269]
| rang gi lha dang bla ma dang |
| dkon mchog gsum dang 'gro ba lnga |
| 'di drug nga yi lha dang ni |
| jo bo yin zhes [2] rtag tu gsung |[270]

---

269 Cf. above lines 149-152
| *'di la mi sbyin 'di la sbyin* |
| *'di la mi dbul 'di la dbul* |
| *thugs ni kun la snyoms gyur pas* |
| *gang la'ang bye brag 'byer mi mdzad* | .

270 Cf. above lines 153-156
| *dkon mchog gsum dang thugs dam lha* |

| lha drug bsten pa khyod la phyag 'tshal lo |
| dpal ldan dge sbyong[271] khyod la phyag 'tshal lo |
| thugs shing snying rje can la phyag 'tshal lo |
| rnal 'byor dbang phyug khyod la phyag 'tshal lo |
| a va dhū ti pa la phyag 'tshal lo |
| rtag tu dbyings na bzhugs la phyag [3] 'tshal lo |
| gzhan dag sdug bsngal gyis gdungs sel la phyag 'tshal lo |
| mar me mdzad dpal ye shes zhabs la phyag 'tshal lo |
| ces lha bla ma byang chub 'od kyis | bla ma rje btsun bhaṃ ga va la bstod pa dge'o | |

maṃ ga laṃ |
| | na mo shā kya mu na ye |
| gang tshe [4] rkang gnyis gtso bo khyod bltams tshe |
| sa chen 'di la gom pa bdun bor nas |
| da ni 'jig rten 'di na mchog ces gsung |
| de tshe mkhas pa kyed la phyag 'tshal ⟨l⟩o |

| dang por̲ dga' ldan lha yi yul nas byon |
| rgyal po'i khab tu yul gyi lhums ⟨s⟩u zhugs̲ |
| lumbi nī yi tshal du thub par bltaṃs |
| [5] bcom ldan lha yi lha la x |

| gzhal yas khang du ma ma brgyad kyis mchod |
| shā kya'i grong du gzhon ⟨n⟩u rol rtser mdzad |
| ser skya'i grong du sa 'tsho khab tu bzhes |
| srid gsuṃ mtshangs mang sku la x |

| grong khyer sgo bzhir skyo ba'i tshul bstan nas |
| mchod rten rnaṃ ngag drung du dbu skra bsil |
| [6] nai ranydza na'i 'graṃ du dka' thub mdzad |
| sgrib gnyis skyon dang bral la x |

| rgyal po'i khab tu glang chen smyon pa btul |
| yangs pa can du spre 'us sbrang rtsi phul |

| *bla ma rnams (3) dang 'gro ba lnga* |
| *'di drug nga yi lha dang ni* | 155
| *jo bo yin zhes rtag tu gsungs* |

271 Or: slong.

| ma ga dhā ru thub pa mngon sans rgyas |
| mkhyen pa'i ye shes 'bar la x |

| vā ra ṇa sī'i chos̲ kyi 'khor ba skor |
| dze ta'i [7] tshal du cho 'phrul chen po bstan |
| rtsva mchog grong du dgongs pa mya ngan 'das |
| thugs̲ nyid nam mkha' 'dra la phyag 'tshal lo |

| de ltar bstan pa'i bdag po bcom ldan gyi |
| mdzad pa'i x |
| ces sags (for: sogs) sangs rgyas kyi mdzad pa bcu gnyis̲ kyi bstod pa slo⟨b dp⟩on dpa' bos mdzad ces grag ⟨g⟩o | | dge'o | |

| | [6a] na mo lo ki shva ra ya
| mkha' mnyam 'gro la mkhyen brtses rab dgongs nas |
| grangs med gsum du tshogs gnyis rab rdzogs te |
| stong gsum mi mdzed zhing gi dpal gyur pa'i |
| 'dren mchog shākya'i tog la phyag 'tshal lo |

| shes rab chen pos de nyid [2] legs rtogs shing |
| brtson pa chen pos go 'phang mchog brnyes pas |
| bstan pa 'di la ston pa gnyis par grags |
| 'phags mchog klu sgrub zhabs la x |

| de sras thu bo dge legs dpal yon can |
| log smra tshar bcad skal ldan rjes bzung ste |
| thar 'dod | [3] rnrams la thar pa'i lam ston pa'i |
| ārya de va'i zhabs la x |

| mkhyen par dkyil 'khor legs bshad 'od stong can |
| rab 'byam shes bya'i mkha' la rab 'phags te |
| dge bshegs gsung rab nyin mor byed pa'i dpal |
| 'phags pa thogs med [4] zhabs la x |

| dgu bcu go dgu 'bum sde'i gzhung rnams kyis |
| gang gis̲ blo gros mgul ba legs brgyan te |
| 'dzam gling 'di na kun mkhyen gnyis par grags |
| mkhas mchog dbyig gnyen zhabs la x |

| phul du byung ba'i blo gros stobs kyis rtsen |
| rmad [5] du byung ba'i yon tan khur gyis brjid |

| log smra 'dam bu'i tshal rnam 'joms mdzad pa'i |
| phyogs kyi glang po'i zhabs la x |

| chos kyi rigs pas chos min pham mdzad cing |
| grags pa'i sgra chen 'jig rten gsum na grags |
| smra ngan mun 'joṃs smra ba'i nyi [6] ma mchog |
| chos kyi gragṣ̱ pa'i zhabs̱ la x |

| 'dul ba rgya mtsho'i dbus na gnas̱ byas nas̱ |
| bslab gsuṃ rnaṃ dag sprul gyi gdengs̱ kas brgyan |
| rnaṃ grol thar pa'̱i nor bu gtsug na mdzes |
| mchog gnyis̱ klu yi dbang po la phyag 'tshal |

| thub pa'i bstan la shing rta'i srol gtong cing
| skye [7] dgu rnaṃs la legs̱ pa'̱i lam ston pa'i |
| 'dzaṃ gling mdzes̱ byed rgyan drug mchog gnyis la |
| rtag tu gus pa'̱i yid kyis phyag 'tshal ⟨l⟩o | |

[the printers' colophon, fol. 6a7]

yig mkhan dpon yig thugs̱ rje ste |
| rkos mkhan dge slong mkha'̱ 'gro yis̱ |
| drin can pha ma la svo pa'̱i |
| 'gro kun tshogs̱ rdzogs̱ sgrib sbyong la |
| glang lo sgang cheb na gnas ⟨s⟩u brkos |
| dge [6b *missing*]

References

TIBETAN SOURCES

Bka'-gdams-kyi rnam-par thar-pa bka'-gdams chos-'byung gsal-ba'i sgron-me (short title: *Bka'-gdams chos-'byung sgron-me*), siglum **G**, dated 1494,[272] author Las-chen Kun-dga' rgyal-mtshan, copy prepared relying on the 17th century blockprint edition[273] in the personal library of Loden Sherap Dagyab Rinpoche, Bonn. The blocks of this edition are listed in the A.D. 1920 *dkar chag* of the printing house of 'Bras-spungs.[274] A copy of this edition is, e.g., also found in the Bihar Research Society, Patna.

The *Bka'-gdams chos-'byung sgron-me* quotes far more lines from the *Bstod-pa brgyad-cu-pa* than all other presently known sources; the lines appear at the following places:

28b3-4 lines 1-8; 28b5-6 lines 10-19, 22-23, 20-21;
29a1-2 lines 50-52; 29a5 lines 24-25; 29a5-6 lines 54-57;
29a6-b1 lines 87-90; 29b2 lines 91-94; 29b3 lines 95-98;

---

272 This date is deduced from the colophon to the book (417a4: *rgyal ba'i bstan pa lo gsum stong drug brgya so gcig 'das pa na*..., "[at a time] when the teaching of the Jina had gone for 3631 years"). According to the calculation system of Atiśa the date of the Buddha's demise is B.C. 2137. But fol. 208a4 of the book refers to the year *me-'brug* (1496) in which Bsod-nams lha'i dbang-po died. A divergent date of composition (viz. A.D. 1505) is given by some other sources, cf. MARTIN 1997: 81, no. 148.

273 JACKSON 1989: 188, no. 1391-1 (B. no. 520): "Edition: by Mi dbang 'Phrin-las-rgya-mtsho, following instructions of the 5th Dalai bla-ma (1617-1682)."

274 Cf. EIMER 1992-3: 28, no. 212. The two-volume reprint of a *Dbu-med* manuscript in B. JAMYANG NORBU, Las-chen Kun-dga'-rgyal-mtshan, *Bka'-gdams-kyi Rnam-par thar-pa Bka'-gdams Chos-'byung Gsal-ba'i Sgron me*. New Delhi 1972, was not available for the preparation of this paper.

29b4 lines 218-219; 29b6 lines 220-221; 30a1 lines 222-225;
30a5 lines 111-112, 115-116; 30b5-6 lines 202-209;
31a4-5 lines 169-174; 31a6 lines 175-176; 32a1 lines 127-128;
32a5 lines 117-120; 32b1-2 lines 129-136; 33a2 lines 315-318;
33a2-4 lines 268-275; 33a4 lines 264-267; 33a5-6 lines 295-302;
33a7-b1 lines 149-152; 33b1 lines 143-148; 33b3 lines 83-86;
33b4 lines 71-74; 33b4-5 lines 309-310; 33b5 lines 252-253;
33b6 lines 254-255; 33b7-34a1 lines 157-158;
34a1-2 lines 159-160; 34a2 lines 99-102; 34a3 lines 238-241;
36b1-2 lines 38-41; 36b2 lines 139-142; 36b4 lines 42-45;
36b6-37a1 lines 46-49; 37a1 lines 147-148; 37a6 lines 137-138;
37b2-3 lines 161-168; 38b5-6 lines 34-37; 39a3-5 lines 276-292;
40b5-6 lines 246-251; 41a4-5 lines 58-67; 41b1-2 lines 68-70;
41b4 line 139; 41b4 lines 175-176; 42a3-4 lines 121-124;
42a5 lines 103-106; 42b6-43a1 lines 198-201;
47b2-3 lines 177-186; 50b4-5 line 334; 51a4-5 lines 226-231;
51a5 lines 234-237; 51b3-4 lines 238-245; 52b3-4 lines 75-80;
54a2 lines 81-82; 54b4-5 lines 153-156;
55b7-56a1 lines 337-344; 56a3-4 lines 345-348;
56b2 lines 260-263; 57a1-2 lines 319-322; 58b4 lines 232-233;
58b4 lines 331-332; 59b2 lines 323-324, 326-328;
60b1 lines 333-336; 60b2 lines 329-330; 62b4-5 lines 210-217;
63a2-4 lines 189-197; 65b4 lines 361-363; 65b4-5 lines 349-352;
91a4-6 lines 177-188.

Bka'-gdams rin-po-che'i chos-'byung rnam-thar nyin-mor byed-pa'i 'od-stong (short title: *Bka'-gdams chos-'byung rnam-thar*), siglum **H**, dated 1484, author (Shā-kya'i dge-slong) Bsod-nams lha'i dbang-po (1423-96),[275] facsimile reprint of a 94 fol. *dbu-med* manuscript in the personal library of Burmiok Athing, Gangtok, formerly belonging to Kaḥ-thog Rig-'dzin Tshe-dbang-nor bu,[276] in: [TSETEN] 1977: 207-394.

Lines of the *Bstod-pa brgyad-cu-pa* appear at the following places:

---

[275] *Bka'-gdams chos-'byung sgron-me*, fol. 208a4, notes that he died in the year *me 'brug*, i.e. 1496, in his 74th year of life. Cf. MARTIN 1997: 79-80, no. 144, as well.

[276] YAMAGUCHI 1970: 163, no. 511-3056.

22a2-5 lines 1-8, 10-19, 22-23, and 20-21; 23a5-6 lines 129-136; 25a1-2 lines 246-251; 25a2-4 lines 58-70.

(*Skyes-bu gsum-gyi nyams-su blang-ba'i*) *Rim-pa thams-cad tshang-bar ston-pa'i byang-chub lam-gyi rim pa* (short title: *Lam-rim chen-mo*), siglum **T**, to be dated 1402, author Tsong-kha-pa Blo-bzang grags-pa (1357-1419), reprint of the Beijing edition of the Collected Works of Tsong-kha-pa in *Tibetan Tripitaka* 1955-1961: vol. 152, pp.1-182 (text no. 6001).

Lines of the *Bstod-pa brgyad-cu-pa* appear at the following places:

3a4-5 lines 1-8, 10-19;	3a7 lines 22-23;	3a7 lines 20-21;
3a8-b1 lines 111-114;	3b1 line 116;	3b7 lines 127-128;
4a3 lines 34-35;	4a6-7 lines 38-41;	4b1-2 lines 42-45;
4b6-7 lines 46-49;	4b8-5a1 lines 145-148;	5a6 line 169;
5a6-7 line 172;	5b1-2 lines 246-251;	5b2-4 lines 58-70;
6a7-b1 lines 161-168;	6b3-4 lines 129-136.	

Jo-bo-rje dpal-ldan mar-me-mdzad ye-shes-kyi rnam-thar rgyas-pa (hereafter: *Rnam-thar rgyas-pa*), siglum **L**, second fascicle of the collection with the marginal title *lam yig*[277] printed in Dga'-ldan phun-thogs-gling (undated).

Lines of the *Bstod-pa brgyad-cu-pa* appear at the following places:

2b5-6 lines 161-168;	3a2 lines 153-156;	10a1-2 lines 248-251;
10a4-5 lines 129-136;	13a4-5 lines 87 and 90;	
18b6-19a1 lines 246-251;		22b1-3 lines 1-8;
23a1-3 lines 10-19, 20-21, and 22-23;		23b4 lines 111-114;
27b5-6 lines 24-25;	28a3 lines 127-128;	36b1-4 lines 276-292;
37b1-2 lines 268-271;	38a5 lines 260-263;	38b1-2 lines 34-37;
40b5-6 lines 58-70;	41b3-4 lines 38-41;	42a1 lines 42-45;
42a3-4 lines 46-49;	42a4-5 lines 334 and 336;	
42b2-3 lines 145-148;	69a5-b1 lines 177-186.	

---

[277] See EIMER 1977: 96-99 and 101-108 (Quellen B 1, 2, and 4), and JACKSON 1989: 168, nos 1303-1 and 1303-2 (B no. 469).

Jo-bo-rje'i bstod-pa brgyad-cu-pa nag-tsho lo-tstshā-ba tshul-khrims rgyal-bas mdzad pa (*bźugs lags so*), siglum **A**, blockprint of 6 fol. dated 1541[278] from Mang-yul Gung-thang. This print comprises lines 1-93, 95-363 of the *Bstod-pa brgyad-cu-pa* (line 94 is therefore, taken from B in the above edition).

References to folios, pages and lines of this blockprint are given in brackets.

Jo-bo-rje'i bstod-pa brgyad-cu-pa nag-tsho lo-tsā bas mdzad pa, siglum **B**, given on fol. 15b1-20a5 of the collection *Legs-par bshad-pa bka'-gdams rin-po-che'i gsung-gi gces-btus nor-bu'i bang-mdzod* (short title: *Bang-mdzod*), 19th century, microfilm copy of the xylograph in the personal library of the late Khri-byang Rin-po-che, it became accessible through the kind help of Loden Sherap Dagyab Rinpoche, Bonn. Another copy of this rare print is found in the Bihar Research Society, Patna.[279] The *Bstod-pa brgyad-cu-pa* covers 363 lines of verse in this text witness.

References to folios, pages and lines of this blockprint are given in parentheses.

Jo-bo rin-po-che dpal-ldan A-ti-sha'i rnam-thar rgyas-pa yongs-grags (short title: *Rnam-thar yongs-grags*), siglum **R**, author Mchims Thams-cad mkhyen-pa, alias Nam-mkha'-grags (died around 1285), occurs in the second fascicle in the first volume (*Pha-chos*) of the *Bka'-gdams glegs- bam*[280] (cover title: *Jo-bo-rje lha-gcig dpal-ldan a-ti-sha'i rnam-thar bla-ma'i yon-tan chos-kyi 'byung-gnas sogs bka'-gdams rin-po-che'i glegs-bam*). The edition here referred to is the recent one coming from the Lhasa Zhol par-khang.[281]

Lines of the *Bstod-pa brgyad-cu-pa* appear at the following places:

---

278 In the colophon the date is indicated as *glang-lo*. Dr Ehrhard deduces from this and the carver's name that the year meant is A.D. 1541.

279 JACKSON 1989: 186, no. 1380 (B. no. 510).

280 Cf. EIMER 1977: 105-106 (Quellen B 3).

281 Siglum "**A**" in EIMER 1977: 72-89.

20b3 lines 129-131; 25b4-6 lines 268-271; 26b3-5 lines 38-49; 32b4-6 lines 276-292; 59a1-2 lines 177-186; 84a3-4 lines 333-336; 87b5-6 lines 319-322.

Deb-ther sngon-po, dated 1476 or 1476-1478, author 'Gos Lo-tsā-ba Gzhon-nu dpal, cf. ROERICH 1949-53.

Byang-chub lam-gyi sgron-ma'i rnam-bshad phul-byung bzhad-pa'i dga'-ston (short title: *Lam-sgron rnam-bshad*), siglum **P**, author Paṇ-chen Lama I. Blo-bzang Chos-kyi rgyal-mtshan (1567-1662), blockprint of 42 fol. prepared in Bkra-shis lhun-po, copy in the Sven-Hedin-Stiftelse, Stockholm, Inv.-No. H.6045, marginal siglum *ḍi*.

Lines of the *Bstod-pa brgyad-cu-pa* appear at the following places:

2a3 lines 50-53; 2b6-3a1 lines 119-122; 3a2-3 lines 145-146; 3a3-4 lines 169-170; 3a5 lines 157 and 176; 3a7-b1 lines 247-250 and 64-67; 3b4 lines 319-322.

Byang-chub lam-gyi rim-pa'i bla-ma brgyud-pa'i rnam-par thar-pa rgyal-bstan mdzes-pa'i rgyan mchog-tu phul-byung nor-bu'i phreng-ba (short title: *Lam rnam*), siglum **Y**, dated 1787, author Yongs-'dzin Tshe-mchog gling-pa Ye-shes rgyal-mtshan (1713-1792), volumes *nga* (4) and *ca* (5) of the Collected Works of Ye-shes rgyal-mtshan, copy prepared relying on the blockprint edition in the personal library of H.H. the Dalai Lama, received through the kind help of Loden Sherap Dagyab Rinpoche, Bonn. Other blockprint copies of this edition are, e.g., found in the Bihar Research Society, Patna, and in the Toyo Bunko, Tokyo.[282]

Lines of the *Bstod-pa brgyad-cu-pa* appear at the following places:

160a2 lines 276-292; 175b3-6 lines 1-8, 10-19, 22-23, and 20-21; 176a6-b1 lines 34-35; 176b4-5 lines 145-148; 200a3-5 lines 177-188.

---

282 JACKSON 1989: 20-21, no. 907 and 909 (B. no. 231 and 233), and YAMAGUCHI 1970: 126-131, no. 371-2664 and -2665.

BIBLIOGRAPHY

JOSÉ IGNACIO CABÉZON and ROGER R. JACKSON (eds.), *Tibetan Literature. Studies in Genre. Essays in Honor of Geshe Lhundup Sopa*. Ithaca, New York 1996 (Studies in Indo-Tibetan Buddhism.)

FRANZ-KARL EHRHARD, *Early Buddhist Block Prints From Mang-yul Gung-thang*. Lumbini 2000. (Lumbini International Research Institute, Monograph Series. 2)

——, "The Transmission of the *Thig-le bcu-drug* and the *Bka' gdams glegs bam*". In: H. EIMER & DAVID GERMANO, *The Many Canons of Tibetan Buddhism. PIATS 2000: Tibetan Studies: Proceedings of the Ninth Seminar of the International Association for Tibetan Studies, Leiden 2000.* Leiden, Boston, Köln 2002. (Brill's Tibetan Studies Library. 2/10), 29-56.

HELMUT EIMER, *Berichte über das Leben des Atiśa* (Dīpaṃkaraśrījñāna). Eine Untersuchung der Quellen. Wiesbaden 1977. (Asiatische Forschungen (hereafter: AF). 51.).

——, *Bodhipathapradīpa*. Ein Lehrgedicht des Atiśa (Dīpaṃkaraśrījñāna) in der tibetischen Überlieferung. Wiesbaden 1978. (AF. 59.).

——, *Rnam thar rgyas pa*. Materialien zu einer Biographie des Atiśa (Dīpaṃkaraśrījñāna). 1. Teil: Einführung, Inhaltsübersicht, Namensglossar. 2. Teil: Textmaterialien. Wiesbaden 1979. (AF. 67.).

——, "The Development of the Biographical Tradition Concerning Atiśa (Dīpaṃkaraśrījñāna)". In: *The Journal of the Tibet Society* 2 (1982), 41-51.

——, "The Hymn of Praise in Eighty Verses. The Earliest Source for the Life of Atiśa". In: *Atish Dipankar Millennium Birth Commemoration Volume (Jagajjyoti*: Sept. 1982 to Jan. 83, Combined and Special Number on Atish Dipankar Srijnan). Calcutta 1983, 1-8.

——, "Nag tsho Tshul khrims rgyal ba's Bstod pa brgyad cu pa in Its Extant Version". In: *Bulletin of Tibetology*, New Series, 1989, No. 1, 21-38.

——, "The Hymn of Praise in Thirty Stanzas. The *Bstod pa sum cu pa* transliterated." In: HEMENDU BIKASH CHOWDHURY (ed.), *Hundred Years of the Bauddha Dharmankur Sabha ⟨The Bengal Buddhist Association⟩*. Calcutta (1992), 182-191.

——, "Der Katalog des Großen Druckhauses von 'Bras-spuṅs aus dem Jahre 1920". In: *Studies in Central & East Asian Religions* 5/6 (1992-3), 1-44.

——, "Hymns and Stanzas Praising Dīpaṃkaraśrījñāna". *Glimpses of the Sanskrit Buddhist Literature*. Vol. 1. Editor: KAMESHWAR NATH MISHRA. Sarnath, Varanasi 1997. (Samyag-Vāk Series. 9), 9-32.

HERBERT V. GUENTHER, *sGam.po.pa, Jewel ornament of Liberation. Dam. chos yid.bzhin.gyi nor.bu thar.pa rin.po.che'i rgyan zhes.bya.ba theg.pa chen.po'i lam.rim.gyi bshad.pa*. For the first time translated from the original Tibetan and annotated. London (etc.) 1959.

DAVID P[AUL] JACKSON, *The 'Miscellaneous Series' of Tibetan Texts in the Bihar Research Society, Patna*. A Handlist. Stuttgart 1989. (Tibetan and Indo-Tibetan Studies. 2.).

——, "The *bsTan rim* ('Stages of the Doctrine') and Similar Graded Expositions of the Bodhisattva's Path". In: CABÉZON / JACKSON 1996: 230-243 ("Chapter 13").

LEONARD W. J. VAN DER KUIJP, "Tibetan Historiography". In: CABÉZON / JACKSON 1996: 39-56 ("Chapter 1").

LOKESH CHANDRA, *Tibetan-Sanskrit Dictionary. Supplementary Volume* 1-7. New Delhi 1992-1994. (Śata-Piṭaka Series 369, 371-372, 374-375, 377-378).

Mahāvyutpatti: YUMIKO ISHIHAMA [and] YOICHI FUKUDA, *A New Critical Edition of the* Mahāvyutpatti. *Sanskrit-Tibetan-Mongolian Dictionary of Buddhist Terminology*. (Tokyo) 1989. (Materials for Tibetan-Mongolian Dictionaries. 1). (Studia Tibetica. 16).

DAN MARTIN, *Tibetan Histories. A Bibliography of Tibetan-Language Historical Works*. D. M. in collaboration with YAEL BENTOR. Foreword by MICHAEL ARIS. London (1997).

R[ICHARD] O. MEISEZAHL, "Der Katalog der Klosterdruckerei *A mčhog dGa' ldan čhos 'khor gliṅ* in Ch'ing-hai (Nordwest-China)," unter Mitwirkung von L. S. DAGYAB RINPOCHE (Bonn). In: *Oriens* 29-30 (1986), 309-333.

PRATAPADITYA PAL and HSIEN-CH'I TSENG, *Lamaist Art: The Aesthetics of Harmony*. Boston 1970.

Tibetan Tripitaka: *The Tibetan Tripitaka. Peking edition. Reprinted under the supervision of the Otani University, Kyoto*. Edited by DAISETZ T[EITARO] SUZUKI. Vol. 1-45 Bkaḥ-ḥgyur. Vol. 46-150 Bstan-ḥgyur. Vol. 151 Dkar-chag. Vol. 152-164 Extra (Btsoṅ Kha Pa/Lcaṅ Skya). Vol. 165-168 Catalogue. Tokyo, Kyoto, Suzuki Research Foundation 1955-1961.

GEORGE N. ROERICH, *The Blue Annals*. Part One. Part Two. Calcutta 1949-53. (Royal Asiatic Society of Bengal. Monograph Series. 7).

R[OLF] A. STEIN, *Les tribus anciennes des marches sino-tibétaines*. Légendes, classifications et histoire. Paris 1961. (Bibliothèque de l'Institut des Hautes Études Chinoises. 15).

[GONPO TSETEN], *Two Histories of the Bka'-gdams-pa Tradition from the Library of Burmiok Athing. Paṇ-chen Bsod-nams-grags pa: Bka' gdams gsar rniṅ* [for *rñiṅ*] *gi chos 'byuṅ yid kyi mdses rgyan (1529), Bsod-nams-lha'i-dban* [for *dbaṅ*]*-po: Bka' gdams rin po che'i chos 'byuṅ rnam thar (1484)*. Gangtok and New Delhi 1977.

ZUIHO YAMAGUCHI, *Catalogue of the Toyo Bunko Collection of Tibetan Works on History*. Tokyo 1970. (Classified Catalogue of the Toyo Bunko Collection of Tibetan Works. 1.).